Contributions to Management Science

More information about this series at http://www.springer.com/series/1505

Sebastian Nielen

Trade Credit and Temporary Employment

How Companies Respond to Capital and Labor Market Frictions

Springer

Sebastian Nielen
Tübingen, Germany

ISSN 1431-1941 ISSN 2197-716X (electronic)
Contributions to Management Science
ISBN 978-3-319-29849-8 ISBN 978-3-319-29850-4 (eBook)
DOI 10.1007/978-3-319-29850-4

Library of Congress Control Number: 2016934039

Printed on acid-free paper

This Springer imprint is published by Springer Nature
The registered company is Springer International Publishing AG Switzerland

Preface

In writing this dissertation I have been lucky to have valuable co-authors. Chapter 2 is co-authored with Werner Bönte. It is already published in the journal Managerial and Decision Economics (Bönte and Nielen 2011) reproduced in this book with permission from John Wiley and Sons. Chapter 3 is solely authored by me. Chapters 4 and 5 are both co-authored with Alexander Schiersch. Chapter 4 is already published in the journal Industrial Relations (Nielen and Schiersch 2014) reproduced in this book with permission from John Wiley and Sons. This doctoral dissertation has been awarded by the University of Wuppertal in June 2014 under its original title "Firms' short-run responses to capital and labor market frictions: the case of trade credit and temporary employment".

Acknowledgments

The biggest thanks go to my parents. Their support enabled me to study Economics. Without their support this thesis would never have been written. I also would like to thank the remaining members of my family, especially my grandparents and my sister. Special thanks also go to my thesis supervisor Werner Bönte for his support in the development process of this thesis. My thanks also go to Alexander Schiersch being co-author of two chapters of the thesis. I also would like to thank all my friends and also my colleagues in Wuppertal, in particular the members of the chair of industrial organization and innovation.

Contents

List of Figures

List of Tables

Chapter 1
Introduction

Not only, but especially in times of financial or economic crises firms have to cope with external shocks. During the economic crises started in 2009 many firms were faced with two kinds of external shocks. First, caused by the financial crises many banks reduce their credit provision. This led to credit constraints especially for small and medium sized firms. Second, caused by the economic crises many firms were confronted with a drop in product demand. During the crises trade credit and temporary employment played a major role in firms' adjustment strategies to cope with those kinds of shocks. Large firms with an easier access to external finance provide trade credit to their smaller business partners. By doing so they helped their smaller business partners to cope with the liquidity shock. Temporary employment was used to adjust the labor force on the reduced product demand during the crisis.

In this dissertation the relationship between firms' short-term response to capital and labor market frictions and their performance is investigated empirically. Figure 1.1 presents the research question of this dissertation.

It is analyzed how firms' short-term responses to capital and labor market friction are related to two different performance measures. The first one is innovation performance and the second one is firm performance. This dissertation analyzes two different firm strategies to deal with external shocks, which are trade credit and temporary employment. There are many different possible relationships could be analyzed to investigate how these strategies to cope with external shocks are related with performance. A relationship which has been already investigated is how temporary employment and innovation performance are related. The results of these studies are mixed. Zhou et al. (2011) find that firms with a relative high share of temporary employees have more sales of imitative new products, while they have lower shares in sales of products which are new to the market. Giannetti and Madia (2013) analyze how different kinds of labor flexibility are related to innovation performance. Their results suggest that internal flexibility is positively related to innovation for high-tech as well as for low-tech firms.

S. Nielen, *Trade Credit and Temporary Employment*, Contributions to Management Science, DOI 10.1007/978-3-319-29850-4_1

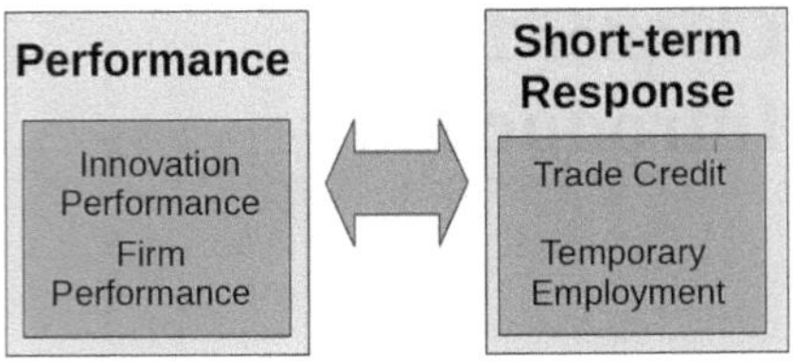

Fig. 1.1 The relationship between firms' short-run responses to capital and labor market frictions and performance

Regarding external flexibility they find a negative effect on innovation performance for high-tech firms. This means that a higher share of temporary employment goes in line with a weaker innovation performance for high-tech firms. Finally Arvanitis (2005) reports a positive relationship between temporary employment and product innovations. Caggese and Cunat (2008) study a different relationship. They analyze how financing constraints affect the use of fixed-term employment. Their theoretical model suggests that firms facing credit constraints make more use of fixed-term employment. An empirical analysis confirms this result.

This dissertation focuses on two different relationships explaining how firms' short-term responses and performance are related. The first one is the relationship between innovation performance and trade credit as a source of short-term finance. The second one is the relationship between the use of temporary employment and firm performance. Both parts consist of two chapters. Within the next two subsections they are explained more detailed.

1.1 Trade Credit and Innovation Performance

The first part of this dissertation includes two chapters analyzing the relationship between innovation performance and trade credit. In both chapters innovation performance is used as explanatory variable. It is measured as the successful introduction of a product innovation. Trade credit is used as dependent variable in both chapters. Two different measures are applied. The first one is the use of trade credit as a source of short term finance, while the second one is a more detailed one. It distinguishes between the demand for and the provision of trade credit. The expected relationship between product innovation and trade credit is illustrated in Fig. 1.2.

The second and third chapter investigate how product innovation and trade credit are related. Theoretical arguments suggest that innovative firms have a higher probability to make use of trade credit. It is argued that this positive relationship is driven by demand as well as supply side. Innovative firms are expected to have a higher probability to demand for trade credit. A supplier has an incentive to provide trade credit especially to customers introducing a product innovation. This relationship is tested empirically in both chapters.

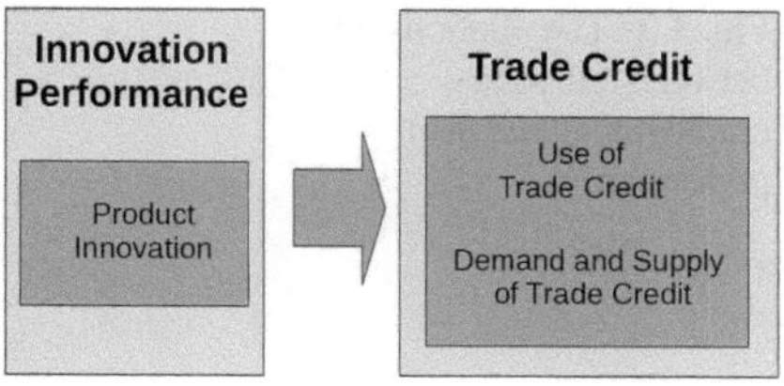

Fig. 1.2 The relationship between innovation performance and trade credit

1.2 Temporary Employment and Firm Performance

Like the first part, the second one also consists of two chapters. In both chapters it is analyzed how the use of temporary employment affects firm performance. To this end between two different kinds of temporary employment are distinguished. The first one is fixed-term employment. Fixed-term employment means that an employee gets a contract only for a certain period. After this period the employee can get another contract or has to leave the firm. The second one is temporary agency work. In case of temporary agency work three different contract partners are involved. The temporary agency worker is hired by a temporary work agency which pays the wage of the temporary agency worker. The work agency sends the temporary agency worker to another firm. The firm lending the temporary agency worker for a certain period has to pay a lending fee to the temporary work agency. This fee includes the wage of the temporary agency work, social security and profits of the temporary work agency. Both kinds of temporary employment are used as independent variables in this part of the dissertation. To measure firm performance, which is the dependent variable in both chapters analyzing the relationship between the use of temporary employment and firm performance, two different measurements are conducted. The first one is labor productivity. It is defined as sales per employee. The second one is unit labor cost. To calculate unit labor cost the sum of all wages including payments for the social security is divided by the number of units produced within the respective time period. The expected relationship between the use of temporary employment and firm performance is illustrated in Fig. 1.3.

The investigation how the use of temporary employment affects firm performance is the content of Chaps. 4 and 5. Based on theoretical suggestions it is argued that the relationship between the use of temporary employment and firm performance is inverse U-shaped. A moderate use of temporary employment should increase firm performance, but an intensive usage is expected to have a negative effect on firm performance.

The rest of this dissertation is organized as follows: Chap. 2 contains the study dealing with the relationship between the introducing a product innovation and the use of trade credit. Chapter 3 uses another measure for trade credit. It distinguishes between the demand for and the availability of trade credit for innovative SMEs. In

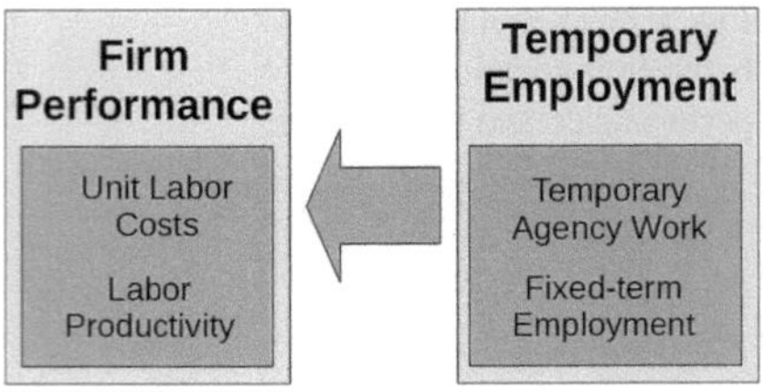

Fig. 1.3 The relationship between temporary employment and firm performance

Chap. 4 the relationship between the use of temporary agency work and unit labor costs is investigated. The relationship between the extent fixed-term employment is used and labor productivity is the purpose of Chap. 5. Finally Chap. 6 summarizes all results of each chapter and gives some ideas for future research on the relationship between firms' short-run responses to capital and labor market frictions and performance.

Chapter 2
Product Innovation, Credit Constraints, and Trade Credit: Evidence from a Cross-Country Study

This chapter studies the relationship between trade credit and innovation. While trade credit is well researched in the finance literature, its link to innovation has been neglected in prior research. We argue that innovative small and medium-sized enterprises (SMEs) are more likely to use trade credit than non-innovative SMEs because of credit constraints and that business partners may have incentives to offer trade credit especially to innovative SMEs. The relationship between innovation and trade credit is empirically examined by using a sample of SMEs from 14 European countries. The results of an econometric analysis confirm a positive relationship between innovation and trade credit. In particular, SMEs with product innovations have a higher probability of using trade credit than other SMEs. Moreover, the results suggest that the effect of product innovation is only statistically significant if SMEs report that access to financing or cost of financing are obstacles for the operation and growth of their businesses. Hence, the results point to the relevance of trade credit as a source of short-term financing for innovative SMEs which are credit constrained.

2.1 Introduction

Many firms allow their customers to delay payment for goods already delivered and by offering trade credit they enable their business partners to cope with liquidity problems. The results of empirical studies show that trade credit is a very important source of short-term external finance.[1] To date, a number of empirical and

[1]Petersen and Rajan (1997), for instance, state that "trade credit is the single most important source of short-term external finance for firms in the United States".

S. Nielen, *Trade Credit and Temporary Employment*, Contributions to Management Science, DOI 10.1007/978-3-319-29850-4_2

theoretical studies analyzed the demand for trade credit and the provision of trade credit: With respect to the demand for trade credit findings suggest that bank credit constrained firms are more likely to resort to trade credit (Biais and Gollier 1997; Petersen and Rajan 1997). Suppliers may be willing to provide trade credit to their customers if they have better information about the business and the credit risk of their customers than banks and if they have less problems to obtain external finance than their customers (Schwartz 1974). Moreover, firms may provide trade credit in order to price discriminate since lengthening the credit period implies a reduction in the effective price (NG et al. 1999). Hence, suppliers may be more willing to offer trade credit to the most price elastic segment of the market, e.g. credit rationed firms, or they may price discriminate because they may have long-term interest in the survival of the business partner (Petersen and Rajan 1997).

This paper contributes to the existing literature by studying the link between trade credit and innovation. We argue that especially *innovative* small and medium-sized enterprises (SMEs) have an incentive to resort to trade credit and at the same time are more likely to be offered trade credit by their business partners. SMEs are per se more likely to be credit constrained than larger firms (Beck et al. 2005) but this may be even more severe for innovative SMEs. If an innovative SME needs short-term external finance it may be credit rationed because banks may have problems to scrutinize the value of the innovative SME and because its intangible assets cannot be used as a collateral for bank loans. Hence, innovative SMEs having problems to obtain sufficient external financing may resort to trade credit. Suppliers may be willing to offer trade credit to an innovative SME because they are better informed about the business situation of the SME than banks and because they are able to assess the future growth potential resulting from product innovations. The supplier may help with trade credit, for instance, if she or he expects that a product innovation will lead to an increase in SME's future sales which may in turn positively affect own future sales given that the business relation will last in the future. This would imply a positive relationship between innovation and trade credit. To the authors' best knowledge the relationship between innovation and trade credit has not been analyzed yet. However, better knowledge about this link is needed to understand how innovative SMEs cope with liquidity problems.

A related strand of literature which dates back to Schumpeter (1942) deals with the role of internal finance for R&D investment. The results of empirical studies suggest that the flow of internal finance is an important determinant of private R&D efforts (Hall 2002; Himmelberg and Petersen 1994). Our research question, however, is quite different. We focus on trade credit as a source of short-term external finance and investigate whether current use of trade credit is related to firms' product innovations in preceding years. Hence, we do not hypothesize that trade credit is a determinant of innovation activities. As pointed out by Miwa and Ramseyer (2008) firms make use of trade credit when they face short-term unexpected exigencies and consequently this type of external finance does not lend itself to financing of long-term oriented R&D investments.

Based on a sample of 4119 small and medium-sized enterprises (SMEs) from 15 European countries obtained from the World Bank Enterprise Surveys we investigate the relationship between innovation and trade credit. Our results suggest that SMEs that upgraded a product line and at the same time introduced a new product line have a higher probability of using trade credit as a source of short-term finance. The probability of using trade credit does not increase, if SMEs solely introduced a new product line. Moreover, a statistically significant relationship between product innovation and trade credit does only exist for SMEs reporting that they face credit constraints whereas this relationship is not significant for firms which do not have problems to obtain debt financing. Furthermore, separate estimations for Germany and transition economies confirm the positive relationship between innovation and trade credit but results suggest that it is stronger for German SMEs.

The paper is structured as follows. In the next section we present theories on trade credit and explain in more detail the link between innovation and trade credit. The third section describes the data set. In the fourth section estimation results are presented and the fifth section discusses the results and concludes.

2.2 Theoretical Framework

In this section we analyze both the motives of innovative SMEs to use trade credit and the motives of their business partners to offer trade credit. We first present existing theories on the demand for trade credit and the provision of trade credit. In doing so, we focus on those theories which are relevant for deriving the link between innovation and trade credit.[2]

2.2.1 Demand for Trade Credit

From a theoretical perspective it is well known that asymmetric information may lead to adverse selection in financial markets (Stiglitz and Weiss 1981). Firms may receive a smaller loan than they desire at the quoted interest rate or among borrowers, some receive loans and others do not although they are observationally identical. Emery (1984) argues that firms facing credit constraints use more trade credit than firms without credit constraints. Empirical support for this hypothesis is reported by Atanasova and Wilson (2003), Danielson and Scott (2004) and Nilsen (2002) who find that credit rationed firms increase their demand for trade credit.

Furthermore, several studies report empirical evidence for a relationship between firm growth rates and the use of trade credit (Cunat 2007; Tsuruta 2008). Cunat (2007) finds that firms with high growth rates tend to increase their use of trade

[2]Excellent surveys of trade credit theories are provided by Petersen and Rajan (1997) and NG et al. (1999). Surveys of empirical results are presented by Summers and Wilson (2003) and Cheng and Pike (2003).

credit relative to other sources of finance in case of liquidity shocks. This can be explained by fast growing firms' need for external finance. This is in line with the finding reported by Howorth and Reber (2003) that fast growing firms tend toward habitual late payment of trade credit. Moreover, the results reported by Tsuruta (2008) suggest that firms with a high level of intangible assets are more likely to use trade credit than firms with low levels of intangible assets.

However, as pointed out by NG et al. (1999, p. 1110) trade credit might be a relatively expensive form of short-term finance. In their sample the most common form of trade credit is "2/10 net 30" which is a combination of a 2 % discount for payment within 10 days and a net period ending on day 30. This implies an annual interest rate of 43.9 %. Hence, firms tend to use trade credit only if they need more short-term external finance than provided by financial institutions. The most relevant explanations for using this relatively expensive kind of external financing are credit rationing by banks and high growth rates implying a need of external finance. Consequently, credit rationed firms are more likely to use trade credit even if they would prefer other sources of short-term external finance (Petersen and Rajan 1994).

2.2.2 Provision of Trade Credit

According to the *financing advantage theory of trade credit* suppliers may have advantages as compared to financial institutions, like banks, in offering credit (Schwartz 1974). Petersen and Rajan (1997) list three major sources for such advantages: advantage in information acquisition, advantage in controlling the buyer, and advantage in salvaging value from existing assets. Having closer relationship with their customers, suppliers are able to gain information about their customers in a cheaper way than banks. Moreover, suppliers use different sources of information than banks do and they are often able to seize delivered goods when customers do not pay. There is an advantage in salvaging if the supplier is able to restore the delivered good before the customer has assimilated it. Another advantage is that a supplier can stop delivering goods to its customer. If the customer has no alternative to get that input, the supplier has the power to threaten its buyers. Financial institutions like banks do not have that kind of power (Bastos and Pindado 2007).

According to the *price discrimination theory of trade credit* offering trade credit to specific customers may be considered as an alternative way to practice price discrimination because trade credit offered to specific buyers is equivalent to a reduction in input price for these buyers. Empirical evidence for the price discrimination theory of trade credit is reported by Pike et al. (2005) and NG et al. (1999). There are two major reasons for using trade credit as a measure to price discriminate (Petersen and Rajan 1997). First, in the *short-run* suppliers may provide trade credit as a form of price reduction to customers with a more elastic demand. Second, suppliers may have a *long-run* incentive to help customers which are in financial trouble. Suppliers may have an interest in the survival of customers to profit from an increase in customer's future demand.

2.2.3 Trade Credit and Innovation

Theoretical and empirical findings suggest that the demand for trade credit is positively related to credit constraints. We argue that especially *innovative SMEs* have a higher probability of using trade credit. First, innovative firms are more likely to be credit constrained than non-innovative SMEs because banks may have problems to scrutinize the firm value if firms' assets are mainly intangible. The results of several empirical studies provide empirical evidence for the hypothesis that innovative firms tend to be credit constrained (Guiso 1998; Hyytinen and Toivanen 2005; Ughetto 2009). Second, small firms are more likely to be credit constrained than large firms irrespective whether they are innovative or non-innovative (Aghion et al. 2007; Beck et al. 2005; Jaramillo et al. 1996). Therefore we expect that innovative SMEs have a higher probability of using trade credit as a source of working capital than non-innovative firms.

Theoretical and empirical findings also suggest that the demand for trade credit is positively related to firm growth. We argue that innovative firms are more likely to use trade credit because they exhibit higher growth rates than non-innovative firms. Almus and Nerlinger (1999) find that new technology-based firms have higher growth rates as compared to non-innovative ones. Coad and Rao (2008) report that being innovative is of crucial importance for fast-growing firms. Roper (1997) finds a positive link between product innovations and output growth while Brouwer et al. (1993) report a positive influence of product innovation on employment growth. Furthermore, results suggest that differences in firm performance measured as sales per employee can be explained by innovation activities. Lööf and Heshmati (2002) find that firms with a high share of sales from new products perform better. Although firm growth is measured in different ways empirical studies point to a positive link between innovation (e.g. product innovation) and firm growth. Hence, innovative SMEs tend to have a higher probability of using trade credit.

According to the financing theory of trade credit suppliers may have an advantage in offering credit to their innovative customers as compared to traditional lenders, like banks, and may therefore provide trade credit to *innovative* customers even when banks do not. Suppliers may offer trade credit to bank credit constrained customers if suppliers have better information about the business of their trading partner than banks. Suppliers may have access to other sources of information than banks which allows them to evaluate the situation of innovative SMEs and enables them to identify customer potentials which cannot be identified by banks. Furthermore, suppliers may use trade credit as a measure to price discriminate and provide financial support especially to *innovative* SMEs. There might be a *short-run* incentive if the demand of innovative customers are more price elastic because of the limited access to bank loans. Suppliers may also have a *long-run* interest in the survival of innovative customers to benefit from a future growth in demand.

To summarize, theory and empirical results let us expect that the demand for trade credit and provision of trade credit are positively related to innovation activities of SMEs. In our empirical analysis we focus on *product* innovations, i.e. new product lines or upgrades of existing product lines. We argue that especially product innovations – new products or upgraded products – tend to be related to future growth. In contrast, the relationship between process innovation and future firm growth is less clear-cut. Reduction in marginal cost may result in an increase in market shares but can also be viewed as a more defensive measure to deal with fierce market competition. Moreover, it might be easier for suppliers to recognize product innovations and to assess their growth effects as compared to process innovations. Both theories, financing advantage theory and price discrimination theory suggest that suppliers tend to offer trade credit rather to innovative than to non-innovative SMEs.

2.2.4 Institutional and Macroeconomic Effects

Beyond product innovation and firm specific characteristics trade credit provision and demand for trade credit may be influenced by institutional and macroeconomic effects. For instance, Fisman and Love (2003) point out the different role of trade credit for firms in countries with highly developed financial markets and firms in countries with less developed ones. Moreover, monetary policy and its transmission channels may differ between countries and this may affect the provision of trade credit and the demand for trade credit (Mateut 2005; Nilsen 2002). Atanasova and Wilson (2003) find that restrictive monetary policy leads to tighter bank credit constraints and therefore tends to increase the demand for trade credit. Empirical studies suggest that industry effects are also relevant since trade credit is more common in some industries than in others. NG et al. (1999) suggest that there exists a lot of variation between industries in using trade credit, but less variation within. In our empirical analysis we take into account differences between countries and industries by controlling for country- and industry-specific fixed effects. One might argue, however, that controlling for fixed unobserved effects is not sufficient. For instance, a positive relationship between product innovation and trade credit may exist in countries with well developed capital markets and innovation systems but may not exist in countries with less developed capital markets and innovation systems or vice versa. Our empirical analysis is based on a sample of 15 European countries which are members of the European Union. However, one might still argue that there are sizable differences between countries with well developed capital markets and innovation systems, such as Germany, on the one hand and transition economies on the other hand. Therefore, we allow for differences between countries by running separate regressions for SMEs from Germany and SMEs from transition economies.

2.3 Data

2.3.1 *Sample*

The data set used in this paper is based on the World Bank Private Enterprise Surveys. World Bank Enterprise Surveys comprise firms from developing as well as developed countries. Most firms in the World Bank survey are small and medium-sized enterprises (SMEs) with less than 250 employees. Hence none of the firms in the sample should have the market power to force its suppliers to grant trade credit to them. Firms are surveyed regarding their perceptions on the major obstacles to enterprise growth, the relative importance of various constraints to increasing employment and productivity, and the effects of a country's business environment on its international competitiveness.[3]

In order to reduce the degree of heterogeneity this study analyzes firms from countries which were already members of the European Union in 2005 or were in the process of becoming members of the EU (Bulgaria and Romania). Moreover, worldwide economic effects should be similar since all companies were surveyed in 2005. Furthermore, this study focuses on firms that are more likely to be affected by financial constraints. All firms share the following characteristics: they are SMEs, the major shareholder of the company is either an individual or a family, the companies are not publicly listed, no company is owned by a government or a state, the largest shareholder or owner of the firm is not a domestic company, a foreign company, a bank or an investment fund. Finally, not all questions are answered by all firms and therefore some firms had to be treated as missing. Our sample comprises 4119 firms from 15 countries.

2.3.2 *Measurement of Variables*

2.3.2.1 Dependent Variable

In the questionnaire, firms are asked to report their *current* sources of working capital and the corresponding shares in total working capital. Possible sources mentioned in the questionnaire are, for instance, internal funds or retained earnings, different types of banks, credit cards or trade credit. To investigate the relationship between innovation and the probability of using trade credit as a source of finance, a dummy variable is generated that takes on the value one if a firm uses trade credit and zero otherwise.

---

[3]For detailed information about the World Bank enterprise surveys and the survey methodology see http://www.enterprisesurveys.org

2.3.2.2 Product Innovations

The World Bank Enterprise Surveys contains information about firm's product innovations during the last 3 years. In particular, firms report whether they have upgraded an existing product line or introduced a completely new one. We distinguish between firms which solely upgraded an existing product line, firms that solely implemented a new product line, and companies that did both. Based on this classification we generate three product innovation dummy variables taking the value one if a firm implemented the respective kind of product innovation during the last 3 years and zero otherwise.

2.3.2.3 Financial Constraints

Firms are asked in the questionnaire whether access to financing (e.g., collateral required or financing not available from banks) or cost of financing (e.g., interest rates and charges) are obstacles for the operation and growth of their business. Firms assessed the respective obstacle on a five point scale ranging from no obstacle, minor, moderate, major to a very severe obstacle. We generate a dummy variable that takes on the value one if a firm reports that one of them is at least a moderate obstacle and zero otherwise.

2.3.2.4 Other Control Variables

To control for several firm characteristics we include the following control variables: the logarithm of the number of employees, which is a proxy for firm size, the logarithm of age, the share of high skilled employees, and purchase of raw material divided by sales. To control for international integration we include the variables share of domestic sales and share of domestic purchases. We use two other groups of binary variables, one for the owner status and one for the legal status. Within the owner status group we distinguish between individual and family owned firms. The reference group are individual owned firms. We also distinguish between four kinds of legal status, sole proprietorship, privately held limited company, partnership or cooperative and foreign owner. Here, sole proprietorship is the omitted group.

2.3.3 Descriptive Statistics

Table 2.1 reports the number of companies in each country and their shares in the total sample. Most firms are from Germany, Poland, Spain, Greece and Ireland. The rest of the SMEs are from Hungary, Romania, Portugal, Czech, Bulgaria, Estonia, Latvia and Lithuania, Slovenia and Slovakia.

Table 2.1 Sample countries: number of observation for each country and share in total sample

Country	Frequency	Percent (%)
Bulgaria	130	3.2
Czech	205	5.0
Estonia	85	2.1
Germany	890	21.6
Greece	384	9.3
Hungary	303	7.3
Ireland	332	8.1
Latvia	81	2.0
Lithuania	80	1.9
Poland	547	13.3
Portugal	250	6.1
Romania	257	6.2
Slovakia	73	1.8
Slovenia	78	1.9
Spain	424	10.3
	4119	100.0

Notes: Only small and medium-sized enterprises (SMEs)

Table 2.2 reports on the distribution of sample SMEs across 20 industries. About 31 % of the SMEs are operating in manufacturing industries, especially in Metals, Machinery and Electronics, Garments, Beverages, Food and Wood, and Furniture industry. Around 69 % are non-manufacturing companies and most SMEs are operating in Retail and Wholesale trade, Construction, Hotels and Restaurants, Transport and Advertising and marketing industry.

To illustrate the importance of trade credit as a source of working capital we compare three external sources of working capital: trade credit, bank loans, and equity. As can be seen from Table 2.3 trade credit is used by 924 firms. Thousand two hundred and seventy-four companies use bank loans and 660 firms use equity. In our sample 22.4 % of all SMEs use trade credit. The share of firms using trade credit exceeds the share of firms using equity and it is not much lower than the share of firms using bank loans. For those SMEs using trade credit the average share of trade credit in total working capital is 37.4 %. This suggests that trade credit is as important as a source of short-term finance as bank loans and equity.

Table 2.4 presents descriptive statistics of the independent variables. As can be seen from the table, SMEs that use trade credit and SMEs that do not use trade credit differ with respect to product innovations. Among the SMEs using trade credit the share of firms that solely upgraded an existing product line is 5.6 % points higher and the share of firms that upgraded and at the same time introduced a new product line is 6.7 % points higher as compared to SMES that do not use trade credit. The difference is negative however for the share of firms that solely introduced a new product line. Furthermore, the share of firms reporting that cost of financing or access to financing are obstacles to the operation and growth of

Table 2.2 Industries: number of observation for each industry and share in total sample

Industry	Frequency	Percent (%)
Textiles and leather	58	1.4
Garments	201	4.9
Food	105	2.6
Beverages	130	3.2
Metals, machinery and electronics	552	11.0
Chemicals and pharmaceutics	26	0.6
Wood and furniture	111	2.7
Non-metallic and plastic materials	64	1.6
Paper	96	2.3
Other manufacturing	22	0.5
Total manufacturing	1265	31
IT services	62	1.5
Construction	544	13.2
Telecommunications	40	1.0
Advertising and marketing	225	5.5
Other services	195	4.7
Retail and wholesale trade	1031	25.0
Hotels and restaurants	318	7.7
Transport	225	5.5
Real estate and rental services	190	4.6
Mining and quarrying	24	0.6
Total non-manufacturing	2854	69

Notes: Number of observations 4119

Table 2.3 External sources of working capital: trade credit, bank loans and equity

	Number of firms	Percent (%)	Share in working capital (%)
Trade credit	924	22.4	37.4
Bank	1274	30.9	40.0
Equity	660	16.0	34.8

Notes: Column (1): Number of SMEs using the respective kind of finance; Column (2): Share in total sample using the respective kind of finance; Column (3): Average share in working capital for SMEs that use the respective kind of finance

their business is about 8.0 % points higher for SMEs using trade credit. For the variables age, number of employees, purchases of raw material divided by sales, main owner family, privately held, limited company and partnership or cooperative differences are positive. The differences for the variables main owner individual, sole proprietorship, share of domestic sales and share of domestic purchases are negative. Except for the variables new product line solely, share of high skilled employees, and foreign owner all differences are statistically significant at least at a five percent level.

Table 2.4 Descriptive statistics of explanatory variables – SMEs without and with trade credit

	Trade credit: No		Trade credit: Yes		
Variable	Mean	Std. Dev.	Mean	Std. Dev.	Difference
Upgraded product line solely	0.197	0.397	0.259	0.438	0.062***
New product line solely	0.063	0.242	0.055	0.228	−0.007
Upgraded and new product line	0.178	0.383	0.246	0.431	0.067***
Access to/cost of financing an obstacle	0.550	0.498	0.630	0.483	0.080***
Age	14.522	14.628	15.889	15.920	1.366**
Number of employees	19.973	35.018	29.863	44.030	7.112***
Purchases of raw material/sales	0.404	0.172	0.424	0.161	0.020***
Share of high skilled employees	0.167	0.265	0.160	0.227	−0.006
Main owner: family	0.178	0.382	0.293	0.456	0.116***
Main owner: individual	0.827	0.378	0.727	0.446	−0.100***
Foreign owner	0.043	0.203	0.048	0.213	0.005
Sole proprietorship	0.440	0.496	0.300	0.458	−0.140***
Privately held, limited company	0.284	0.451	0.332	0.471	0.049***
Partnership or cooperative	0.276	0.447	0.368	0.483	0.092***
Share of domestic sales	0.942	0.182	0.926	0.197	−0.016**
Share of domestic purchases	0.786	0.343	0.741	0.345	−0.046***

Notes: Column (1) and (2): Means and standard deviations reported for SMEs without trade credit; Column (3) and (4): Means and standard deviations reported for SMEs with trade credit; Column (5): Difference between SMEs with and without trade credit
$^*p < 0.1$; $^{**}p < 0.05$; $^{***}p < 0.01$

2.4 Estimation Results

Our data set allows us to identify SMEs using trade credit as a source of working capital but it does not contain information about the firms providing trade credit. Hence, we are not able to estimate the "demand" and the "supply" equations of trade credit separately. Instead, we test our main hypothesis of a positive relationship between product innovation and trade credit by estimating a binary probit regression model which may be interpreted as the reduced form of trade credit "demand" and "supply". The dependent variable takes on the value one if a firm uses (receives) trade credit and zero otherwise. The right hand side variables are the product innovation variables, the dummy variable reflecting financial constraints, and various control variables such as size, age, legal form of the firm, owner status or export/import measures. Moreover, we include country and industry dummy variables to control for unobserved industry- and country-specific fixed effects.

Table 2.5 reports the marginal effects of the explanatory variables on the probability of using trade credit. Marginal effects instead of estimated coefficients of the probit model are reported because the former are more straightforward to interpret. Our estimation results reported in Column (1) of Table 2.5 suggest that upgrading an existing product line has a positive and statistically significant marginal effect on the probability of using trade credit. Upgrading an existing and at the same time

Table 2.5 Probit estimation results: relationship between the probability of using trade credit, credit constraints, and product innovation

Variable	(1)	(2)	(3)	(4)	(5)
Upgraded product line solely	0.0478***	0.0755***	0.0092	0.1331***	0.00452
	(0.0182)	(0.0258)	(0.0254)	(0.0415)	(0.0330)
New product line solely	0.0036	−0.0062	0.0307	−0.0457	0.0340
	(0.0289)	(0.0400)	(0.0433)	(0.0441)	(0.0595)
Upgraded and new product line	0.0693***	0.0947***	0.0340	0.0775**	0.1086***
	(0.0204)	(0.0275)	(0.0298)	(0.0366)	(0.0379)
Obstacle: access to/cost of finance	0.0830***	–	–	–	–
	(0.0132)				
Log (age)	−0.0240**	−0.0249	−0.0232*	−0.0497**	−0.0068
	(0.0097)	(0.0142)	(0.0130)	(0.0205)	(0.0186)
Log (employees)	0.0441***	0.0374***	0.0525***	0.0399***	0.0294**
	(0.0063)	(0.0087)	(0.0090)	(0.0120)	(0.0117)
Share of high skilled employed	0.0196	−0.0158	0.0524	0.1049*	−0.0699
	(0.0281)	(0.0400)	(0.0393)	(0.0612)	(0.0520)
Purchase of raw material/sales	−0.0239	0.0358	−0.0931	−0.0338	0.0668
	(0.0487)	(0.0710)	(0.0660)	(0.1227)	(0.0872)
Main owner: family	0.0756***	0.0699***	0.0849***	0.0889**	0.0662*
	(0.0184)	(0.0251)	(0.0276)	(0.0404)	(0.0320)
Foreign owner	−0.0211	−0.0095	−0.0295	−0.0008	−0.0437
	(0.0308)	(0.0482)	(0.0385)	(0.0621)	(0.0630)
Privately held, limited company	0.0293	0.0834***	−0.0312	0.1459***	0.0697*
	(0.0208)	(0.0308)	(0.0271)	(0.0566)	(0.0382)
Partnership or cooperative	0.0651***	0.0938***	0.0259	0.1307***	0.0894***
	(0.0193)	(0.0265)	(0.0276)	(0.0424)	(0.0346)
Share of domestic sales	−0.0591	−0.0902*	−0.0276	−0.0969*	−0.0476
	(0.0374)	(0.0496)	(0.0580)	(0.0522)	(0.0981)
Share of domestic purchases	−0.0491**	−0.0714**	−0.0171	0.0112	−0.1347***
	(0.0215)	(0.0295)	(0.0309)	(0.0397)	(0.0408)
Industry fixed effects	YES	YES	YES	YES	YES
χ^2	62.91***	57.97***	33.51**	14.72*	29.87***
Country fixed effects	YES	YES	YES	YES	YES

(continued)

Table 2.5 (continued)

Variable	(1)	(2)	(3)	(4)	(5)
χ^2	202.27***	158.19***	64.16***	32.34***	126.74***
Pseudo R^2	0.1245	0.1568	0.1049	0.1906	0.1478
Wald χ^2	500.25***	370.88***	173.39***	120.08***	244.89***
Number of observations	4119	2338	1781	814	1519

Notes: Marginal effects are reported. For binary coded variables, the result expresses the impact of a discrete change of the variable from 0 to 1. The reference category for product innovation variables is companies without product innovation. Dependent variable: Trade credit yes/no. Robust standard errors in parentheses

*p < 0.1; **p < 0.05; ***p < 0.01. Column (1): all SMEs are included; Column (2): only SMEs with financing problems are included; Column (3): only SMEs without financing problems are included; Column (4): only SMEs with financing problems operating in the manufacturing sector are included; Column (5):only SMEs with financing problems operating in non-manufacturing sectors are included

implementing a new product line is associated with an increase in the probability of using trade credit by 6.93 % points and this marginal effect is statistically significant at the one percent level. SMEs that solely introduced a new product line are not more likely to use trade credit as compared to SMEs without product innovation. Facing financing problems (limited access to or high cost of external finance) has also positive and statistically significant impact on the probability of using trade credit as a source of working capital. The second and the third columns report the results for SMEs with financing problems and SMEs without such problems. Our results show that the effect of upgrading a product line and implementing a new one is only statistically significant for firms with financing problems. Again, solely introducing a new product line does not have any statistically significant effect. Moreover, the estimated marginal effects of the product innovation variables increase if the empirical analysis is restricted to the sample of SMEs reporting financing problems. For firms without financing problems marginal effects of the innovation variables are statistically insignificant. The last two columns report marginal effects for manufacturing and non-manufacturing firms with financing problems. For manufacturing firms with financing problems solely upgrading a product line and doing both upgrading and introducing a new product line have positive and statistically significant marginal effects on the probability of using trade credit, while for non-manufacturing firms with financial problems only SMEs that did both upgrading an existing product line and at the same time implementing a new one have a higher probability of using trade credit. Hence, our main hypothesis of a positive relationship between product innovation and the probability of using trade credit is confirmed by our empirical results. However, firms that solely implement a new product line without upgrading an existing one are not more likely to use trade credit.

Control variables have also statistically significant effects on the probability of using trade credit. In all model specifications the number of employees has a positive and statistically significant impact on the probability of using trade credit which indicates that among SMEs larger firms are more likely to use trade credit. In contrast, the sign of the marginal effect of age is negative. Especially younger firms may be affected by financial constraints and may therefore have to resort to trade credit to overcome such restrictions. Huyghebaert (2006) finds that even business start-ups make use of trade credit and that trade credit theories are also relevant for start-ups (Huyghebaert et al. 2007).

Furthermore, we find that family owned firms tend to have a higher probability of using trade credit than SMEs owned by individuals. This might be explained by network effects which may increase the probability of receiving trade credit. Family owned firms may have better opportunities to use social networks as compared to SMEs owned by individuals. Social network effects may also explain the finding that firms with the legal status partnership or cooperative have a higher probability of using trade credit than SMEs with the legal status sole proprietorship.

In order to check the robustness of our results we perform additional regressions. As explained in Sect. 2.1 we cannot exclude the possibility that countries differ with respect to the strength of the link between innovation and trade credit. One might expect, for instance, that the link between product innovation and the probability of using trade credit may be different for SMEs from Germany and SMEs from transition countries. We therefore run separate regressions for German SMEs and SMEs from transition economies. For each group we estimate one model using all firms and one model which is based on the subsample of firms with financing problems. The first two columns of Table 2.6 report the results for German SMEs and the last two columns present the results for the firms from transition economies.

For German SMEs we find a positive and statistically significant marginal effect of upgrading an existing product line and introducing a new product line at the same time. The estimated value of the marginal effect implies that the probability of using trade credit is 14.6 % points higher for SMEs with upgraded products and newly introduced product lines. Column (2) reports the results for SMEs with financing problems. For these firms the marginal effect of innovation is even higher. SMEs with an upgraded product line have a 12.4 % points higher probability of using trade credit and for firms that did both upgrading an existing product line and implementing a new product line the probability is 38.8 % points higher. Estimation results based on the sample of SMEs from transition economies confirm the positive link between innovation and trade credit. SMEs that upgraded an existing product line and implemented a new product line have a higher probability of using trade credit.

Table 2.7 reports the results of additional robustness checks. Column (1) reports the estimation results using alternative measures for credit constraints. As an alternative measures we generate dummy variables for each level of the two financing obstacles (access to finance, cost of finance). In column (1) SMEs reporting that access to financing and cost of financing are no obstacles are the reference group for the respective kind of obstacle. Compared to the model using the simple measure the marginal effects of the marginal effects of product innovation variables are hardly affected. Again SMEs upgrading an existing product line and upgrading an existing in combination with implementing a new product line are more likely to use trade

Table 2.6 Probit estimation results: relationship between the probability of using trade credit and product innovation – differences between German SMEs and SMEs from transition countries

Variable	(1)	(2)	(3)	(4)
Upgraded product line solely	0.0364	0.124**	0.0506**	0.0824**
	(0.0410)	(0.0592)	(0.0245)	(0.0321)
New product line solely	−0.0740	0.105	0.0183	0.00597
	(0.112)	(0.164)	(0.0340)	(0.0421)
Upgraded and new product line	0.146**	0.388***	0.0564**	0.0449
	(0.0600)	(0.0647)	(0.0246)	(0.0292)
Obstacle: access to/cost of to finance	0.220***	–	0.0500***	–
	(0.0337)		(0.0170)	
Log (age)	−0.0287	−0.00112	−0.0301**	−0.0299*
	(0.0267)	(0.0423)	(0.0147)	(0.0180)
Log (employees)	0.0662***	0.0173	0.0322***	0.0341***
	(0.0210)	(0.0326)	(0.00743)	(0.00929)
Share of high skill employed	−0.0486	−0.0759	0.0271	0.00930
	(0.0963)	(0.175)	(0.0336)	(0.0410)
Purchase of raw material/sales	−0.280**	−0.136	0.0854	0.138
	(0.117)	(0.183)	(0.0734)	(0.0934)
Main owner: family	0.165***	0.0889	0.0514*	0.0456
	(0.0465)	(0.0670)	(0.0279)	(0.0332)
Foreign owner	0.0625	−0.00685	−0.0245	−0.00824
	(0.101)	(0.139)	(0.0350)	(0.0514)
Privately held, limited company	0.0959	0.178**	0.0704**	0.0966**
	(0.0604)	(0.0811)	(0.0330)	(0.0440)
Partnership or cooperative	0.0542	0.154**	0.0645***	0.0816***
	(0.0453)	(0.0672)	(0.0249)	(0.0314)
Share of domestic sales	0.328	0.151	−0.0525	−0.0733*
	(0.217)	(0.317)	(0.0360)	(0.0444)
Share of domestic purchases	−0.110	−0.128	−0.0378	−0.0388
	(0.0932)	(0.135)	(0.0238)	(0.0299)
Industry fixed effects	YES	YES	YES	YES
χ^2	37.67***	43.74***	28.01*	26.84*
Country fixed effects	NO	NO	YES	YES
χ^2			42.63***	15.54**
Pseudo R^2	0.1524	0.1581	0.1245	0.1174
Wald χ^2	155.62***	102.54***	188.60***	129.57***
Number of observations	888	456	1839	1228

Notes: Marginal effects are reported. For binary coded variables, the result expresses the impact of a discrete change of the variable from 0 to 1. The reference category for product innovation variables is companies without product innovation. Dependent variable: trade credit yes/no; Robust standard errors in parentheses

*p < 0.1; **p < 0.05; ***p < 0.01; Column (1): only German SMEs are included; Column (2): only German SMES with financing problems are included; Column (3): only SMEs from transition countries are included; Column (4): only SMEs with financing problems from transition countries are included

Table 2.7 Additional estimation results

	(1)	(2)	(3)	(4)
Variable	Trade credit	Trade credit	Trade credit	Access to cost of finance
Upgraded product line solely	0.0445**			0.115***
	(0.0182)			(0.0208)
New product line solely	0.0016			0.0417
	(0.0285)			(0.0350)
Upgraded and new product line	0.0679***			0.1518***
	(0.0204)			(0.0213)
Process innovation		0.0230		
		(0.0157)		
Invested in R&D			0.0259	
			(0.0254)	
Obstacle: access to/ cost of finance		0.0888***	0.0918***	
		(0.0131)	(0.0136)	
Access minor obstacle	0.0585***			
	(0.0222)			
Access moderate obstacle	0.0951***			
	(0.0239)			
Access major obstacle	0.0753***			
	(0.0280)			
Cost minor obstacle	0.1000***			
	(0.0240)			
Cost moderate obstacle	0.0828***			
	(0.0242)			
Cost major obstacle	0.0384			
	(0.0269)			
Controlled for firm characteristics	YES	YES	YES	YES
Industry fixed effects	YES	YES	YES	YES
χ^2	67.35***	58.33***	59.73***	32.07**
Country fixed effects	YES	YES	YES	YES
χ^2	202.54***	213.60***	208.51***	255.28***
Pseudo R^2	0.1354	0.1205	0.1259	0.0907
Wald χ^2	530.11***	484.14***	464.67***	461.84***
Number of observations	4119	4098	3822	4119

Notes: Marginal effects are reported. For binary coded variables, the result expresses the impact of a discrete change of the variable from 0 to 1. The reference category for innovation variables is companies without innovation. Robust standard errors in parentheses

*$p < 0.1$; **$p < 0.05$; ***$p < 0.01$. Column (1): Dummies for the degree of credit rationing are included; Column (2): Dummy included which takes on the value one if a SME introduced a process innovation and zero otherwise; Column (3): Dummy included which takes on the value one if a SME invested in R&D and zero otherwise; Column (4): Dependent variable is the dummy variable for credit constraints

credit. Column (2) reports the results of an estimation where a dummy variable is included which takes on the value one if a firm introduced a process innovation in the last 3 years and zero otherwise. As discussed in Sect. 2.1 we expect that product innovations are related to the probability whereas the introduction of process innovations is less likely to be related to the use of trade credit. This is confirmed by the statistically insignificant marginal effect of the process innovation variable. Column (3) reports the results of an estimation where a dummy variable is included which takes on the value one if a SME conducted R&D in the year 2004 and zero otherwise. Again the estimated marginal effect is statistically insignificant. Hence, SMEs conducting R&D are not more likely to use trade credit and/or their business partners may not be willing to provide trade credit unless the research activities lead to product innovations. The last column of Table 2.7 provides empirical evidence for the relationship between product innovations and the probability of being credit constrained. Here, the dependent variable is the dummy variable reflecting financial constraints. We find positive and statistically significant marginal effects for all product innovation variables except implementing a new product line solely. This result is in line with the results reported by Ughetto (2009) who finds a positive link between product innovations and the probability of being credit constrained.

To summarize, our results suggest a positive relationship between product innovation and the probability of using trade credit. Furthermore, this positive link does only exist for credit constrained SMEs. These results are robust to changes in econometric specification, do hold for various sub-samples and are hardly affected by the inclusion of additional variables. Our results do also suggest that this relationship does only exist for product innovations whereas process innovations and R&D activities are not positively linked to the probability of using trade credit.

2.5 Discussion and Conclusion

This study contributes to the existing literature by studying the relationship between trade credit and innovation. We argue that innovative SMEs are more likely to use trade credit and to be offered trade credit by business partners. The demand for trade credit is related to product innovation since it is likely that innovative SMEs are credit constrained and may therefore resort to trade credit as a source of short-term external finance. Suppliers may have an incentive to offer trade credit to *innovative* SMEs because they are better informed than banks and because they can assess the growth potential of innovative SMEs.

Our main hypothesis of a positive relationship between innovation and trade credit is confirmed by the results of our empirical analysis. In particular, our results suggest that SMEs which upgraded an existing product line in the preceding years are more likely to use (receive) trade credit than other SMEs. The probability of using trade credit is not higher, however, if a SMEs solely introduced a completely new product line but did not upgrade an existing product line. Moreover, our results suggest that process innovations and R&D activities are not positively related to trade credit. One explanation for these results may be supplier expectations. While suppliers may be able to predict the demand for customers' upgraded products it is much more difficult to predict future demand for completely new product lines and to assess the effects of process innovations and R&D activities. Hence, trade credit does not seem to be related to innovation in general but the positive relationship seems to be restricted to incremental product innovations.

The results also suggest that the positive relationship between product innovation and trade credit does only exist for the subsample of SMEs reporting that access to financing and cost of financing are obstacles for the operation and growth of their businesses. This result can be explained by the incentives of SMEs to use trade credit. Depending on the terms of trade credit it can be an expensive source of working capital (NG et al. 1999). Therefore, innovative SMEs which are not credit constrained simply may not have an incentive to use trade credit whereas credit constrained SMEs may use it in addition to bank loans or in the most extreme case as "financing of last resort". Finally, our results indicate that the positive relationship between product innovation and trade credit is stronger for German SMEs than for SMEs from transition economies which may point to the relevance of institutions, like legal systems or implicit institutions.

Taken together, our results suggest that trade credit is an important source of short-term external finance for innovative SMEs facing liquidity problems due to limited access to financing and cost of financing. Hence, trade credit offered by business partners may help innovative SMEs to cope with financial problems, to run their businesses, and to survive. This source of finance becomes even more important in times of financial crisis when banks reduce their credit supply and innovative SMEs are at risk to run out of bank credit.

Since this study is based on a cross-sectional data set, time dimension is not considered in our econometric analysis. Therefore, the results should be interpreted as prima facie evidence for a positive relationship between product innovation and trade credit. Future research should analyze the time dimension of this relationship by using panel data and it should examine the effects of product innovations on trade credit supply and demand separately. Moreover, it would be worthwhile to investigate the relationship between innovation, short-term and long-term financing within an integrated framework.

Chapter 3
Product Innovation and Trade Credit Demand and Supply: Evidence from European Countries

This chapter addresses the relationship between product innovation and the demand for and supply of trade credit. It is argued that introducing a product innovation is positively linked with trade credit demand as well as the availability of trade credit from business partners. Using a sample covering SMEs from 24 European countries this relationship is tested empirically. Basically the estimation results confirm both hypotheses. First, SMEs introducing a product innovation have a higher probability to demand for trade credit. Second, the availability of trade credit from business partners is also higher compared to non-innovative SMEs. This relationship is found to be stronger for small and young firms. Hence, this study points to the role of trade credit as a source of short-term finance for small and young innovative firms.

3.1 Introduction

If suppliers allow their customers to pay already delivered goods after a certain time they provide trade credit to them. In the short-run trade credit is a very important source of finance (Petersen and Rajan 1997). Demand and supply of trade credit have already been investigated by a large number of theoretical as well as empirical studies. Regarding trade credit demand results of other studies suggest that firms facing credit constraints by banks increase their demand for trade credit (Biais and Gollier 1997; Schwartz 1974). With respect of trade credit supply the following is found in the existing literature. Firms may use trade credit as a mechanism to practice price discrimination among their customers since varying trade credit conditions could be used instead of direct price discrimination (NG et al. 1999). Moreover, suppliers may help their customers to cope with short-term liquidity problems because they have an interest in survival of their customers (Petersen and Rajan 1997).

S. Nielen, *Trade Credit and Temporary Employment*, Contributions to Management Science, DOI 10.1007/978-3-319-29850-4_3

The link between innovation output and trade credit as a source of short-term finance finds only little observance in the literature. To the authors best knowledge empirical literature on the relationship of product innovation and the demand and provision of trade credit is rare. Bönte and Nielen (2011) study the relationship between the use of trade credit and product innovation. Using firm level data and applying probit regression models they find that firms introducing a product innovation have a higher probability to make use of trade credit as a source of short term finance. However, the data used in this study does not allow to distinguish between provision and demand of trade credit.

This study contributes to the existing literature by analyzing the relationship between introducing a product innovation and trade credit demand and provision for European SMEs. It is argued that especially innovative small and medium sized firms resort to trade credit because they have to cope with fundamental financial constraints. Banks have problems to scrutinize the value of innovative SMEs and therefore restrict their credit provision to them. Moreover, innovative SMEs have relative high levels of intangible assets which cannot be used as collateral for bank loans. From the supply side there are also arguments why trade credit is especially relevant for innovative SMEs. First, a supplier has an advantage in providing credit to innovative customers compared to banks because of a closer relationship with the customer. Therefore, the supplier is able to gain information about the situation of the innovative firm cheaper than the bank. Second, the supplier has an incentive to help its innovative customers to cope with short term financing problems via offering trade credit. Since the product innovation may lead to higher growth rates for the customer the supplier can profit from an increase in future demand. Hence we expect a positive link between introducing a product innovation and the demand for and availability of trade credit.

Using data from the Flash Eurobarometer on SMEs access to finance the expected positive link between product innovation and trade credit demand and supply is tested empirically. In general the estimation results confirm both hypotheses. SMEs reporting the introduction of a product innovation have a significant higher probability to demand for trade credit. Moreover, firms implemented a product innovation have also a higher probability that the willingness of business partners to provide trade credit has increased. The results suggest that product innovations are positively related to trade credit demand as well as trade credit supply. But estimations for different subsamples provide mixed results. The positive link between product innovation and the provision of trade credit is only found for SMEs being active in service sectors and for SMEs located in countries being a part of the low Finance Index group. Regarding the demand for trade credit the positive link with product innovation is only confirmed by estimations manufacturing SMEs and SMEs located in high Finance Index countries. Estimation results focusing on young SMEs show a stronger relationship between introducing a product innovation and trade credit demand and willingness of business partners to provide trade credit for those firms.

The remainder of the paper is structured as follows. In Sect. 3.1 relevant theories and empirical evidence regarding trade credit are presented. Using them the link between product innovation and trade credit demand and supply is explained and the hypotheses are derived. Section 3.2 introduces the data set, the variables that are used and provides some descriptive statistics. The estimation results are purpose of the fourth section and the last section concludes.

3.2 Theoretical Framework

In this section theories regarding trade credit demand and supply as well as results of empirical studies are presented. The focus is on theories explaining how product innovation and trade credit demand and supply are related. Afterwards the discussed theories and empirical studies are used to explain the relationship between product innovation and the demand for and provision of trade credit.

3.2.1 Demand for Trade Credit

The main incentive regarding trade credit demand is credit rationing by banks because of asymmetric information in financial markets leading to adverse selection (Stiglitz and Weiss 1981). As a result firms receive less bank loans than they want or they get no external finance from banks at all. As pointed out by a theoretical study of Emery (1984) firms facing credit constraints increase their demand for trade credit. Empirical support for a positive relationship between credit constraints and the demand for trade credit is found by Atanasova and Wilson (2003) and Danielson and Scott (2004). They report that firms facing credit rationing by banks try to overcome it by substituting bank credit with trade credit. This is in line with the findings of Nilsen (2002) that in case of a tight monetary policy the demand for trade credit increases.

Another important influence for trade credit demand is firm growth. Firms with high growth rates tend to use more trade credit (Cunat 2007; Tsuruta 2008). The reason for this is that fast growing firms need more short-term finance for their growth (Carcia-Teruel and Martinez-Solano 2007). Therefore, they prefer finance which is rapidly available (Tsuruta 2012). Banks need more time to screen potential lenders compared to suppliers which have the advantage of day by day monitoring. Hence, fast growing firms have a higher demand for trade credit. This is in line with the findings of Howorth and Reber (2003). They report that fast growing firms tend toward habitual late payment of trade credit.

3.2.2 Trade Credit Demand and Product Innovation

Findings of theoretical and empirical studies show that credit constraints increase demand for trade credit. We argue that innovative SMEs are especially affected by credit rationing and therefore have a higher demand for trade credit for three reasons. First, small firms in general are more likely to face credit constraints independent whether they are innovative or not (Aghion et al. 2007; Beck et al. 2005; Jaramillo et al. 1996). Second, innovative firms have a relative high level of intangible assets compared to non-innovative firms. The relative high share of intangible assets leads to fundamental problems for banks to scrutinize the value of an innovative SME. This results in higher credit constraints for innovative firms compared to non-innovative ones. Empirical evidence for the relationship between credit constraints and innovation is reported by Guiso (1998) and Ughetto (2009). Third, the existing literature also suggest that credit rationing is positively linked to firm growth. Several empirical studies point out that innovative firms have higher growth rates than non-innovative firms (Almus and Nerlinger 1999; Coad and Rao 2008). Roper (1997) reports that product innovation and output growth are positively related. Moreover, the study of Brouwer et al. (1993) suggest that employment growth is influenced by product innovations in a positive way. Finally Lööf and Heshmati (2002) find that firms with a high share of sales from new products perform better. Firms introducing a product innovation have higher growth rates and are therefore more likely to face credit rationing by banks.

Summing up, we argue that innovative SMEs are more likely to face credit constraints. Small firms in general are more likely to be affected by credit rationing and the relative high share of intangible assets and their high growth rates lead to higher credit constraints for innovative SMEs. The positive link between a higher level of intangible assets and the use of trade credit is confirmed by the study of (Tsuruta 2008). Hence, innovative SMEs have a higher probability to demand for trade credit compared to non-innovative SMEs.

Hypothesis one: *SMEs introducing a product innovation have a higher probability to demand for trade credit.*

3.2.3 Provision of Trade Credit

In this subsection two theories regarding trade credit supply are discussed: financing advantage theory of trade credit and price discrimination theory of trade credit. Regarding financing advantage theory it is argued that suppliers have an advantage in providing credit to their customers compared to banks (Schwartz 1974). This advantage has three sources: advantage in information acquisition, advantage in controlling the buyer and advantage in slaving value from existing assets (Petersen and Rajan 1997). Because of a closer relationship with their customers suppliers are able to gain information about the situation of their customers in a cheap and easy way. Moreover, suppliers also have the opportunity to seize delivered goods when the customer does not pay. Furthermore a supplier is able to punish its customers by stopping the supply of inputs (Bastos and Pindado 2007). This is especially the case when the customer depends on the input of a specific supplier. This is in line with the findings of a theoretical study of Jain (2001). She reports that even banks prefer indirect lending via suppliers to other firms by providing trade credit to them when the monitoring costs for the bank are too high. The redistribution theory of bank credits via suppliers is supported by the empirical findings of Rodriguez-Rodriguez (2006). Moreover, Carcia-Teruel and Martinez-Solano (2010) find that firms with a better access to capital markets provide more trade credit to their customers.

According the price discrimination theory providing trade credit is used as a form of price discrimination. Instead varying prices among customers terms of trade credit are varied, because changes in the credit period are equivalent to changes in effective prices (NG et al. 1999). Petersen and Rajan (1997) list two reason why trade credit could be used to price discriminate. First, in the short run suppliers may have an incentive to provide trade credit to customers with a more price elastic demand. This equals a price reduction for these customers and sales to them will increase in the short run. Second, suppliers have an incentive to help customers to overcome financial problems via providing trade credit to them. In the long run the supplier can profit from increasing demand of these customers. In the short run the supplier invests in the survival of its customers by offering trade credit to them and in the long run the supplier profit from the demand of the respective customer. Empirical evidence for the use of trade credit as an alternative way to practice price discrimination is found by Pike et al. (2005) and NG et al. (1999).

3.2.4 Trade Credit Supply and Product Innovation

In this study it is argued that both above presented theories regarding trade credit supply are especially relevant for SMEs introducing a product innovation. The advantage for suppliers in providing credit to its customers compared to banks is more relevant for innovative firms. A supplier may be able to evaluate the potential of a product innovation and therefore is willing to provide credit even when banks are not. Price discrimination theory of trade credit is also more relevant for innovative SMEs. Suppliers have an incentive to help especially innovative customers to cope with financing constraints, because innovative firms have higher growth rates and this will lead to an increase in future demand for the supplier. Hence, the supplier's interest that the customer survives is higher if the customer has introduced a product innovation. Therefore innovative firms are more likely to gain help from their suppliers via offering trade credit.

Financing advantage and price discrimination theory of trade credit are especially relevant for innovative SMEs. The advantage in providing credit over banks is higher for innovative SMEs than for non-innovative SMEs. The incentive to help customers to cope with short-term liquidity problems is also higher if the customer as introduced a product innovation. Therefore we expect a positive relationship between introducing a product innovation and the willingness of business partners to provide trade credit.

Hypothesis two: *SMEs introducing a product innovation have a higher probability to be offered trade credit from business partners.*

3.3 Data

3.3.1 Sample

This study uses data from the Flash Eurobarometer on SME Access to finance in the European Union and other European countries. The survey is conducted on behalf of the Directorate General for Enterprise and Industry of the European Commission and the European Central Bank. The aim of this survey is to provide information on the kind of finance European firms use and what problems they have to obtain their finance. Therefore the dataset contains information of firms from all 27 countries which are a member of the European Union. Furthermore Iceland, Croatia and Norway are also included in the data. Because of a perfect correlation with at least one dependent variable Estonia, Latvia, Hungary, Croatia, Malta and Norway have to be excluded from the analysis. This study focuses on the relationship between product innovation and trade credit demand and supply for small and medium sized firms which make financial decisions by their own. Therefore, all firms have the following characteristics. Number of employees for each firms is less than 250 and the owner is an individual or a family. All firms are not publicly listed or owned by a government or state. Largest shareholder or owner is not a domestic company, foreign company, bank or investment fund. All firms are surveyed in 2009. The final sample comprises 2698 SMEs from 24 European countries.

3.3.2 Measurement of Variables

3.3.2.1 Dependent Variables

In this study the relationship between product innovation and trade credit demand and supply is investigated. Therefore two different dependent variables are calculated. In the questionnaire firms were asked whether they applied for different kinds of finance including trade credit or not. For trade credit demand a dummy variable is created that takes the value of one if a firm has applied for trade credit within the past 6 month and zero otherwise. Firms were also asked whether the availability of different sources of finance has improved, remained unchanged, deteriorated, or were not used over the past 6 month. For trade credit supply a dummy variable is created that takes the value of one if the availability of trade credit from business partners has increased within the past 6 month and zero otherwise.

3.3.2.2 Product Innovation

In the questionnaire firms are asked about their innovation activities. Four different kinds of innovations are distinguished: product innovation, process innovation, organization innovation, and marketing innovation. Since the focus of this study is the relationship between product innovation and trade credit demand and supply, a dummy variable is created taking the value of one if a firm introduced a new or significantly improved product or service to the market during the past year and zero otherwise.

3.3.2.3 Control Variables

The questionnaire includes a question regarding the availability of bank loans in the past 6 month. Possible answers are that the availability of bank loans had increased, was unchanged, had deteriorated or the firm did not want to use bank loans or they were not applicable. For each of the possible answers a separate dummy variable was created which takes the value of one if the firm give the respective response and zero otherwise. Another group of dummy variables covers turnover growth over the past 6 month. Three different scenarios are possible: turnover increased, remained unchanged or decreased. For each scenario a separate dummy variable is created taking the value of one if the firm reports the respective scenario and zero otherwise.

Further control variables are the logarithm of age and the logarithm of number of employees as a proxy for firm size. Additionally a dummy variable for ownership is included. This dummy variable takes the value of one if a firm is owned by a family and zero otherwise. The respective reference category is a dummy variable for single person owned firms. Trade credit demand and supply may also be affected by macro-economic effects. The role of trade credit is different in countries with highly developed financial markets compared to countries with less developed ones (Fisman and Love 2003). Moreover, monetary policy and its transmission channels also affect trade credit (Atanasova and Wilson 2003; Mateut 2005; Nilsen 2002). To capture these effects country specific fixed effects are included in all models. NG et al. (1999) find that there is less variation within but more variation between industries in using trade credit. To take this into account industry specific fixed effects are also included as controls.

3.3.3 Descriptive Statistics

Table 3.1 shows the number of observation for each country and the share in total sample. Most SMEs in the sample are located in Poland followed by the United Kingdom and Germany. Within this table all countries are separated into two groups. This classification is based on the SME Access to Finance Index (SMAF). This index is based on three sub-indicies covering informations regarding access to debt finance, access to equity finance and perceptions of SMEs in relation to accessing

Table 3.1 Countries: number of observation for each country and share in total sample

Country	Finance index	Freq.	Percent	Cum.
Low finance index group				
Romania	64.19	93	3.45	3.45
Slovakia	85.82	67	2.48	5.93
Spain	85.98	169	6.26	12.19
Ireland	86.91	46	1.7	13.89
Poland	88.74	226	8.38	22.27
Bulgaria	89.08	89	3.3	25.57
Cyprus	92.48	61	2.26	27.83
Czech	93.63	113	4.19	32.02
Greece	94.74	123	4.56	36.58
High finance index group				
United Kingdom	96.51	220	8.15	44.73
Germany	96.54	217	8.04	52.77
Denmark	96.75	68	2.52	55.29
Netherlands	97.61	102	3.78	59.07
Belgium	98.17	103	3.82	62.89
Portugal	99.07	163	6.04	68.93
Austria	100.88	109	4.04	72.97
France	100.89	181	6.71	79.68
Slovenia	101.50	69	2.56	82.24
Italy	101.73	163	6.04	88.28
Lithuania	101.73	32	1.19	89.47
Luxembourg	106.06	58	2.15	91.62
Finland	107.80	71	2.63	94.25
Sweden	113.66	97	3.6	97.85
Iceland		58	2.15	100
Total		2698	100	

Notes: Only small and medium-sized enterprises (SMEs); For Iceland no information regarding the finance index is available

Table 3.2 Industries: number of observation for each industry and share in total sample

Industry	Freq.	Percent	Cum.
c. mining and quarrying	66	2.45	2.45
d. manufacturing	405	15.01	17.46
e. electricity, gas and water supply	11	0.41	17.87
f. construction	352	13.05	30.91
g. wholesale and retail trade; etc.	871	32.28	63.19
h. hotels and restaurants	165	6.12	69.31
i. transport, storage and communication	160	5.93	75.24
k. real estate, renting and business activities	457	16.94	92.18
m. education	28	1.04	93.22
n. health and social work	36	1.33	94.55
o. other community, social and personal	147	5.45	100
Total	2698	100	

Notes: Only small and medium-sized enterprises (SMEs)

finance.[1] The reference point of this index corresponds to the EU-average in 2007, meaning that the value for the EU average in 2007 equals 100 %. Since all firms in our sample are asked in the year 2009, the classification used in this study is based on the finance index values of 2009. We distinguish between countries with high and with low level of the finance index. Low finance index countries are countries with a finance index below the average of our finale sample. This group contains Romania, Slovakia, Spain, Ireland, Poland, Bulgaria, Cyprus, Czech and Greece. The remaining countries are part of the high finance index group which contains all countries with a finance index above the average.

Table 3.2 contains the number of observations for each industry and the respective share in total sample. Most firms operate in the sectors of wholesale and retail trade followed by real estate, renting and business activities. The third largest industry is manufacturing.

Table 3.3 provides descriptive statistics for all dependent and independent variables. About 5.6 percent of all firms in the sample report that the availability of trade credit from business partners has increased in the past 6 month and about 13 % applied for trade credit during the same period. The average age in the sample is about 19 years and the average size is about 16 employees. The share of family owned firms is about 59 %, while the remaining firms are owned by single person owners.

[1]For detailed information see: http://ec.europa.eu/enterprise/policies/finance/data/enterprise-finance-index/sme-access-to-finance-index/index_en.htm

Table 3.3 Descriptive statistics

Variable	Mean	Std. Dev.
Trade credit supply	0.0560081	0.2299765
Trade credit demand	0.1276307	0.3337348
Product innovation	0.3577733	0.4794263
Turnover increase	0.2345553	0.4237925
Turnover same	0.2861507	0.4520374
Turnover decrease	0.479294	0.4996559
Bank loans increased	0.0841819	0.2777076
Bank loans unchanged	0.3815343	0.4858457
Bank loans deteriorated	0.3143245	0.4643251
Bank loans not used	0.2199593	0.4142891
age	19.23557	22.52909
Employment	15.87848	27.48351
Owner: family	0.5933469	0.4912925

Notes: Only small and medium-sized enterprises (SMEs); Number of Observations: 2698

3.4 Results

In this section estimation results for trade credit demand and supply are presented. For both dependent variables separate probit models are estimated. Because they are easier to interpret, marginal effects are reported instead of coefficients. First, for both dependent variables a model is estimated without including the control variables concerning bank loan availability and turnover growth. This is done because both variable groups are affected by product innovation as pointed out in Sect. 3.1. Including them as control variables may capture a part of the effect of product innovation on trade credit demand and supply. Second, models including all control variables are estimated to check whether there is still an effect for product innovations on both dependent variables. Probit models for two different size classes (micro and small sized firms) are also presented. Finally we estimate a probit model only including young firms for trade credit demand and supply. In doing so we follow the definition for young firms to be in the age up to 10 years as used in the study of Oliveira and Fortunato (2006).

To check the validity of our base line results separate models for manufacturing and service industries as well as for two different country groups are reported. The first group contains firms located in countries with a finance index blow the average in our sample. Firms located in a country having a finance index above the average are in the second group. Finally robustness checks are carried out to check the validly of the results. First, we estimate a bi-probit regression model including the demand as well as the supply equation to check whether this affects our results. Finally, we estimate a logit model for trade credit supply taking into account low shares of observations taking the value of one in the dependent variable, because only about 5.6 percent of all firms in our sample report that the availability of trade credit has increased.

3.4.1 Trade Credit Demand

Table 3.4 provides the estimation results reporting marginal effects of a probit regression model for trade credit demand. The first column shows the results without including control variables that could be driven by the product innovation variable. The estimated marginal effect is about 2.5 percentage points and it is significant at the 5 % level. Including also the control variables that could be a function of the product innovation variable reduces the marginal effect to 1.9 percentage points

Table 3.4 Probit estimation results: relationship between trade credit demand and product innovation

Variable	(1)	(2)	(3)	(4)	(5)
Product innovation	0.0247**	0.0187*	0.0105	0.0836***	0.0524***
	(0.0120)	(0.0113)	(0.0136)	(0.0290)	(0.0207)
Turnover increase		0.0558***	0.0344*	0.0804*	0.0488*
		(0.0188)	(0.0207)	(0.0455)	(0.0300)
Turnover decrease		0.0386***	0.0189	0.0734**	0.0526**
		(0.0137)	(0.0160)	(0.0340)	(0.0248)
Bank loans: unchanged		0.0172	0.0137	0.0672	−0.0086
		(0.0201)	(0.0240)	(0.0541)	(0.0332)
Bank loans: deteriorated		0.0732***	0.0805***	0.1494***	0.0746**
		(0.0241)	(0.0311)	(0.0612)	(0.0387)
Bank loans: not use		−0.0367*	−0.0189	−0.0543	−0.0330
		(0.0181)	(0.0225)	(0.0518)	(0.0302)
Log(age)	−0.0177**	−0.0120*	−0.0105	−0.0195	−0.0336*
	(0.00714)	(0.0069)	(0.0087)	(0.0185)	(0.0189)
Log(employment)	0.0306***	0.0258***	0.0214**	0.0167	0.0286***
	(0.0048)	(0.0046)	(0.0099)	(0.0291)	(0.0079)
Owner: family	0.0172	0.0160	0.0078	0.0358	−0.0079
	(0.0118)	(0.0111)	(0.0131)	(0.0279)	(0.0197)
Industry fixed effects	YES	YES	YES	YES	YES
Country fixed effects	YES	YES	YES	YES	YES
Pseudo R^2	0.1400	0.1711	0.1650	0.1580	0.1788
Number of observations	2698	2698	1487	765	931

Notes: Marginal effects are reported. For binary coded variables, the result expresses the impact of a discrete change of the variable from 0 to 1. Robust standard errors in parentheses
* $p<0.1$; ** $p<0.05$; *** $p<0.01$. Column (1): all SMEs are included; Column (2): all SMEs are included; Column (3): only micro firms; Column (4): only small firms; Column (5): only young firms

which is significant at the 10 % significance level. The third column provides results only including micro sized firms and the fourth column only includes small firms excluding micro sized firms. In both models all control variables are included. Only in the sample consisting of only small firms the marginal effect is significant. The respective marginal effect is about 8.4 percentage points which is of economic importance. Finally the last column includes only young firms. Here the estimated marginal effect is about 5 percentage points. It is significant at the 1 % significance level and the magnitude is higher than the one found in the whole sample.

Table 3.5 provides estimation results on the relationship between product innovation and trade credit demand for different subsamples. The first column includes only manufacturing firms and the second one contains only service firms. Columns three and four provides the results for firms located in low and high level finance index countries, respectively.

Table 3.5 Probit estimation results: relationship between trade credit demand and product innovation

Variable	(1)	(2)	(3)	(4)
Product innovation	0.1330***	0.0009	0.0108	0.0202*
	(0.0443)	(0.0127)	(0.0226)	(0.0120)
Turnover increase	0.1388**	0.0593***	0.0759**	0.0450***
	(0.0778)	(0.0228)	(0.0415)	(0.0187)
Turnover decrease	0.0777	0.0240	0.0488*	0.0343**
	(0.0547)	(0.0156)	(0.0275)	(0.0147)
Bank loans: unchanged	0.0574	0.0099	0.0257	0.0141
	(0.0714)	(0.0241)	(0.0395)	(0.0211)
Bank loans: deteriorated	0.0185	0.0889***	0.1011**	0.0538**
	(0.0715)	(0.0308)	(0.0426)	(0.0277)
Bank loans: not use	−0.1091	−0.0398	−0.0807**	−0.0142
	(0.0556)	(0.0213)	(0.0346)	(0.0201)
Log(age)	−0.0181	−0.0040	0.0072	−0.0159***
	(0.0259)	(0.0084)	(0.0193)	(0.0060)
Log(employment)	0.0578***	0.0251***	0.0222**	0.0273***
	(0.0180)	(0.0056)	(0.0096)	(0.0048)
Owner: family	0.0226	0.0158	0.0666***	−0.0160
	(0.0423)	(0.0133)	(0.0230)	(0.0122)
Industry fixed effects	NO	YES	YES	YES
Country fixed effects	YES	YES	YES	YES
Pseudo R^2	0.1789	0.1813	0.1529	0.1712
Number of observations	339	1797	987	1646

Notes: Marginal effects are reported. For binary coded variables, the result expresses the impact of a discrete change of the variable from 0 to 1. Robust standard errors in parentheses
* p<0.1; ** p<0.05; *** p<0.01. Column (1): only manufacturing; Column (2): only service; Column (3): low finance index; Column (4): high finance index

The estimated marginal effect for introducing a product innovation is relative high in magnitude for manufacturing SMEs and is also highly significant. For service SMEs the respective marginal is also positive as expected, but not significant. Within the different country groups only the marginal effect for the subsample including only SMEs located in a country with a high level of the finance index provides a significant marginal effect for product innovation.

Regarding the control variables the following is found. Firms reporting increasing turnover in the last 6 month have a higher probability to apply for trade credit compared to firms which report unchanged turnover (unchanged turnover is the reference group). The same is found for firms reporting decreased turnover. Deteriorated bank loan availability is highly positively related with the probability to apply for trade credit. The respective marginal effect is significant in nearly all models. Age has a negative marginal effect in all models except the model for the low finance index countries, but is only significant in some of them. Size is positively related with the possibility to apply for trade credit. The marginal effect of the dummy variable owner family is positive in most of the models but only significant in the model for low finance index countries.

In general a positive relationship between implementing a product innovation and trade credit demand is confirmed by the estimation results. The positive relationship between introducing a product innovation and the demand for trade credit is especially found for small and for young firms. Moreover, firms facing credit rationing by banks are also found to have a higher probability to apply for trade credit.

3.4.2 Trade Credit Supply

Table 3.6 shows the results for trade credit supply. Again marginal effects after probit models are reported. Column one provides the estimation results without including control variables that could be affected by the product innovation variable. The estimated marginal effect is about 2.6 percentage points and is significant at the 1 % level. Including all control variables leads to a smaller marginal effect of about 1.6 percentage points, significant at the 5 % significance level. For both size classes the estimated marginal effects are also positive as expected, but not significant. In the last column the results for young firms are reported. The respective marginal effect is highly significant and more than two times larger than the one estimated marginal effect using the whole sample.

Estimation results of the relationship between introducing a product innovation and trade credit supply for different subsamples are reported in Table 3.7. Surprisingly, the estimated marginal effect for product innovation is negative for the manufacturing subsample. However, the respective estimated marginal effect is insignificant. For service industries as well as for SMEs located in countries with a finance index being below the average significant marginal effects are found. Both have the expected positive sign.

Table 3.6 Probit estimation results: relationship between trade credit supply and product innovation

Variable	(1)	(2)	(3)	(4)	(5)
Product innovation	0.0258***	0.0159**	0.0135	0.00866	0.0392***
	(0.00928)	(0.00744)	(0.00938)	(0.00887)	(0.0159)
Turnover increase		0.0190*	0.01123	0.0166	0.0172
		(0.0101)	(0.0117)	(0.0154)	(0.0191)
Turnover decrease		−0.00009	−0.0221**	0.0203*	−0.0042
		(0.00791)	(0.0101)	(0.0126)	(0.0179)
Bank loans: unchanged		−0.0842***	−0.0719***	−0.0607***	−0.0875***
		(0.00943)	(0.0113)	(0.0144)	(0.0172)
Bank loans: deteriorated		−0.0626***	−0.0522***	−0.0397***	−0.0820***
		(0.00757)	(0.00961)	(0.0105)	(0.0175)
Bank loans: not use		−0.0637***	−0.0637***	−0.0393***	−0.0836***
		(0.00673)	(0.00957)	(0.0070)	(0.0127)
Log(age)	−0.00528	−0.00248	−0.00753	−0.00158	−0.0122
	(0.00522)	(0.00478)	(0.00605)	(0.00567)	(0.0140)
Log(employment)	0.00167	−0.00108	0.00101	−0.0128	0.0061
	(0.00353)	(0.00300)	(0.00666)	(0.0101)	(0.0063)
Owner: family	−0.00586	−0.00227	−0.0097	0.01019	−0.0106
	(0.00876)	(0.00749)	(0.00869)	(0.00822)	(0.0147)
Industry fixed effects	YES	YES	YES	YES	YES
Country fixed effects	YES	YES	YES	YES	YES
Pseudo R^2	0.0540	0.1518	0.1987	0.1912	0.1573
Number of observations	2698	2698	1564	733	865

Notes: Marginal effects are reported. For binary coded variables, the result expresses the impact of a discrete change of the variable from 0 to 1. Robust standard errors in parentheses
* p<0.1; ** p<0.05; *** p<0.01. Column (1): all SMEs are included; Column (2): all SMEs are included; Column (3): only micro firms; Column (4): only small firms; Column (4): only young firms

Regarding the control variables the following can be stated. Increased turnover is positively related to the probability that the willingness of business partners to provide trade credit has increased. However, the respective marginal effect is only significant in some models. The marginal effect of turnover decrease is negative in all models except the model for small firms. Interestingly, for both size classes we find opposite effects of decreasing turnover which are both significant. For micro-sized firms the estimated marginal effect is negative, implying that suppliers are not willing to provide more trade credit to their customers when they show a negative growth in turnover. The opposite is true for small firms. In all models for trade credit supply all bank loan variables have negative marginal effects which are in most cases highly significant. Age, size measured by the number of employees, and the variable owner family have no significant effect on the probability that the availability of trade credit from business partners has increased in the past 6 month in most of the models.

Table 3.7 Probit estimation results: relationship between trade credit supply and product innovation

Variable	(1)	(2)	(3)	(4)
Product innovation	−0.00069	0.0173**	0.0351**	0.0072
	(0.0153)	(0.00826)	(0.0162)	(0.0081)
Turnover increase	−0.00390	0.0310***	0.0209	0.0169*
	(0.0234)	(0.0137)	(0.0250)	(0.0113)
Turnover decrease	0.0118	−0.00074	0.0012	−0.0015
	(0.0208)	(0.00858)	(0.0179)	(0.0090)
Bank loans: unchanged	−0.0710***	−0.0730***	−0.0978***	−0.0785***
	(0.0246)	(0.0107)	(0.0163)	(0.0132)
Bank loans: deteriorated	−0.0343*	−0.0480***	−0.0875***	−0.0477***
	(0.0175)	(0.00815)	(0.0169)	(0.0082)
Bank loans: not use	−0.0140	−0.0579***	−0.0856***	−0.0513***
	(0.0188)	(0.00731)	(0.0128)	(0.0079)
Log(age)	0.00216	−0.00377	−0.0019	−0.0039
	(0.0124)	(0.00472)	(0.0130)	(0.0044)
Log(employment)	0.0095	−0.00385	−0.0089	0.0024
	(0.00713)	(0.00302)	(0.0066)	(0.0032)
Owner: family	−0.0509***	−0.00278	−0.0065	−0.0028
	(0.0245)	(0.00730)	(0.0159)	(0.0078)
Industry fixed effects	NO	YES	YES	YES
Country fixed effects	YES	YES	YES	YES
Pseudo R^2	0.1877	0.1839	0.1287	0.1796
Number of observations	255	1844	987	1625

Notes: Marginal effects are reported. For binary coded variables, the result expresses the impact of a discrete change of the variable from 0 to 1. Robust standard errors in parentheses
* $p<0.1$; ** $p<0.05$; *** $p<0.01$. Column (1): only manufacturing; Column (2): only service; Column (3): low finance index; Column (4): high finance index

In general the expected positive link between product innovation and the provision of trade credit by suppliers is confirmed by the empirical results. This link is found to be relative strong for young firms and for firms located in countries with a relative low finance index. In contrast to the results found for trade credit demand, deteriorated availability of bank loans is negatively related to trade credit supply.

3.4.3 Robustness Checks

In this subsection two different robustness checks are carried out. First, coefficients of separate probit models for trade credit demand and supply are compared with coefficients of a bivariate probit model estimating the demand and supply equation simultaneously. This is done because there could be omitted variables like for example management ability influencing trade credit demand and supply and then both equations are not unrelated and should be estimated simultaneously. The second and last robustness check is only done for the trade credit supply model. Because about only 5.6 percent of all SMEs in the sample report that the availability of trade credit from business partners has increased, coefficients of a logit model are compared with the coefficients resulting from a rare event logit. The rare events logistic regression model takes into account low share of observations taking the value of one in the dependent variable (King and Zeng 2001). The results of the robustness checks are shown in Table 3.8.

Both robustness checks confirm the results of our base line models. Estimating both equations simultaneously has only a very small effect on the coefficients compared to the coefficients resulting from separate probit models for trade credit demand and supply. Therefore the reported marginal effects in our baseline results are not affected by that kind of bias. The same is found for the second robustness check. Estimated coefficients of the rare events logit model are quite similar compared to the ones resulting from a standard logit regression model.

3.5 Conclusion

This study analyzes the relationship between product innovation and trade credit demand and supply. Regarding trade credit demand it is argued that innovative SMEs have a higher probability to be affected by credit rationing by banks. This credit rationing leads to funding credit constraints for innovative SMEs and therefore they have a higher probability to demand for trade credit compared to non-innovative SMEs. Thus, a positive relationship between introducing a product innovation and trade credit demand is expected. There are also arguments for a positive relationship between product innovation and the availability of trade credit from business partners. Suppliers may provide trade credit especially to innovative customers because they have an advantage in providing credit to them compared to banks. Moreover, a supplier has an incentive to help innovative fast growing customers to cope with financing constraints because he can profit from an increase in future demand. Hence, trade credit provision from suppliers is also expected to be positively related with introducing a product innovation. Both links are tested empirically in this study.

In general the empirical analysis confirms both hypotheses. Innovative SMEs are found to have a higher probability to demand for trade credit. Implementing a product innovation is also positively linked to the probability that the willingness of business partners to provide trade credit has increased. Hence, the results point out to the relevance of trade credit as a source of short term finance for innovative SMEs. Estimation results focusing on young firms show that both links are found be stronger for young innovative SMEs. The same is true for the relationship between introducing a product innovation and the demand for trade credit in case of small

Table 3.8 Robustness checks

Model	Bi-probit		Probit		Re-logit	Logit
Dependent variable	Provision	Demand	Provision	Demand	Provision	Provision
Variable	(1)	(2)	(3)	(4)	(5)	(6)
Product innovation	0.185**	0.119*	0.184**	0.120*	0.361**	0.369**
	(0.087)	(0.071)	(0.087)	(0.071)	(0.181)	(0.184)
Turnover increase	0.203*	0.324***	0.209*	0.327***	0.400*	0.421*
	(0.112)	(0.101)	(0.112)	(0.101)	(0.230)	(0.234)
Turnover decrease	−0.006	0.244***	0.001	0.252***	−0.016	−0.008
	(0.104)	(0.089)	(0.104)	(0.089)	(0.224)	(0.227)
Bank loans: unchanged	−1.145***	0.118	−1.152***	0.112	−2.134***	−2.207***
	(0.122)	(0.128)	(0.121)	(0.127)	(0.244)	(0.248)
Bank loans: deteriorated	−0.955***	0.436***	−0.957***	0.431***	−1.717***	−1.781***
	(0.117)	(0.128)	(0.117)	(0.127)	(0.220)	(0.223)
Bank loans: not use	−1.260***	−0.264*	−1.265***	−0.269*	−2.384***	−2.483***
	(0.149)	(0.149)	(0.149)	(0.149)	(0.320)	(0.325)
Log(age)	−0.032	−0.081*	−0.030	−0.079*	−0.052	−0.053
	(0.058)	(0.045)	(0.058)	(0.045)	(0.122)	(0.124)
Log(employment)	−0.012	0.172***	−0.013	0.170***	−0.022	−0.026
	(0.037)	(0.030)	(0.037)	(0.030)	(0.077)	(0.078)
Owner: family	−0.022	0.109	−0.027	0.107	−0.091	−0.093
	(0.091)	(0.076)	(0.090)	(0.076)	(0.188)	(0.191)
Industry fixed effects	YES		YES	YES	YES	YES
Country fixed effects	YES		YES	YES	YES	YES
Pseudo R^2			0.1518	0.1711		0.1507
Number of observations	2698		2698	2698	2698	2698

Notes: Robust standard errors in parentheses (except column 5 where the robust option is not available)
* p<0.1; ** p<0.05; *** p<0.01. Column (1): bi-probit results for trade credit provision; Column (2): bi-probit results for trade credit demand; Column (3): probit results for trade credit provision; Column (4): probit results for trade credit demand; Column (5): rare event logit results for trade credit provision; Column (6): logit results for trade credit provision

firms. The respective marginal effects are highly significant and are also relative high in magnitude. This is in line with the findings of Huyghebaert (2006) und Huyghebaert et al. (2007) that trade credit is especially relevant for young firms and start-ups. Furthermore, Ogawa et al. (2013) find that trade credit is especially relevant for young and small firms.

Regarding the relationship between bank loan availability and the demand for and provision of trade credit opposing results are found. Decreasing availability of bank loans is positively linked with the demand for trade credit, but negatively with the willingness of suppliers to provide trade credit.

However, the results should be interpreted with caution. The estimation results are based on cross sectional data and could therefore be affected by unobserved fixed effects which may be correlated with introducing a product innovation and trade credit. A purpose for further research could be to use panel data containing information about firms innovation activities and information about sources of short-term financing (e.g. trade credit) to take into account unobserved heterogeneities affecting product innovation and trade credit demand and supply. Moreover, more research on the role of trade credit as a source of short-term finance for (innovative) young firms and start-ups is necessary.

Chapter 4
Temporary Agency Work and Firm Competitiveness: Evidence from German Manufacturing Firms

This chapter addresses the relationship between the utilization of temporary agency workers by firms and their competitiveness measured by unit labor costs, using a rich, newly built, data set of German manufacturing enterprises. The analysis is conducted by applying different panel data models while taking the inherent selection problem into account. Making use of dynamic panel data models allows us to control for firm specific fixed effects as well as for potential endogeneity of explanatory variables. The results indicate an inverse U-shaped relationship between the extent that temporary agency workers are used and the competitiveness of firms.

4.1 Introduction

Temporary agency work is a tool that allows firms to adjust labor input on short notice. In Germany, it has become increasingly important since 1994, when regulations concerning temporary employment were relaxed. Between 1994 and 2007, the number of temporary agency workers in Germany quadrupled from roughly 175,000 to over 700,000. However, it must be noted that despite this growth, only 2.4 % of the working population in 2007 were hired by temporary agencies (Schmidt and Wuellerich 2011). The growth in the use of temporary agency workers is by no means only a German phenomenon; it can be observed throughout the industrialized world. The share of temporary agency workers in Japan, for example, grew in the active population by more than 1.3 percentage points to 2.1 % between 2000 and 2007. In European countries like Switzerland, Austria, Finland and Italy,

---

This chapter was originally co-authored with Alexander Schiersch and has been reproduced here with permission from John Wiley and Sons.

S. Nielen, *Trade Credit and Temporary Employment*, Contributions to Management Science, DOI 10.1007/978-3-319-29850-4_4

the growth in temporary agency work was 0.7 percentage points over the same period (Eichhorst et al. 2010).

The increasing importance of temporary work is of growing interest to economists. Although there is an extensive discussion on this form of employment, the discussion is driven by a labor market perspective. Only few studies have taken into account or explicitly analyzed the effect of temporary agency work on firm performance. Arvanitis (2005), Kleinknecht et al. (2006) and Bryson (2007) investigate the effects of the utilization of temporary agency work for Switzerland, the Netherlands and Great Britain. All three studies, while making use of pooled OLS, find no significant effects on sales, value added or sales per capita. In addition, Beckmann and Kuhn (2009) as well as Hirsch and Mueller (2012) study the question for the German case. Both studies apply panel data models to account for time variant and invariant heterogeneity on data from the IAB establishment panel to analyze the effect of temporary agency work on value added and sales. Both papers find a hump-shaped relationship between temporary agency work and productivity. Finally, Beckmann and Kuhn (2012), also using the IAB establishment panel, analyze which strategy pays off: The use of temporary agency work to increase input flexibility or to screen for new productive workers. Also controlling for the self-selection problem, they find negative effects for the flexibility strategy on firm performance, i.e. sales per capita.

This study extends the existing literature on the effects of temporary employment on firm performance in two ways: We apply panel data models on a rich, newly combined, panel data set of more than 26,000 German manufacturing enterprises. The advantage of this data set is that it contains annual data for the use of temporary agency work instead of date data. Moreover, the study is focusing on competitiveness, which is measured by unit labor costs (ULC). This has the advantage that not only the effect of temporary employment on productivity is taken into account, but also potential cost effects. Furthermore, the analysis explicitly controls for the inherent selection problem into using temporary agency work, since some firms systematically do not use this instrument. To offset the strict exogeneity assumption of explanatory variables and to account for dynamic effects, the analysis is making use of system GMM in addition to OLS and the fixed effect approach.

Almost all econometric results confirm our hypothesis of an inverse U-shaped relationship between the share of temporary agency work and firm competitiveness. Only when temporary agency work is modeled as being endogenous, this pattern is not found for the entire data set. However, when testing the hypothesis separately for industries and industry groups, the inverse U-shaped relationship is found even for the model taking into account the potential endogeneity of the Share variables in five out of eleven industry groups covering more than 40 % of all observations.

The remainder of the paper is organized as follows. The next section reviews the broad range of discussions in connection with temporary agency work and fixed-term employment. From this, we develop the hypothesis to be tested. The third section presents related studies. In the fourth section, the data are introduced and first descriptive statistics are presented. The results of the analysis are the subject of the fifth section and the last section provides some conclusions.

4.2 Literature and Hypothesis Development

In this section, we summarize the literature on the effects of temporary agency work on employees and firms, using it to derive our hypothesis about the relationship between firm performance and temporary agency work.

One argument put forth to explain the use of temporary agency work by firms is that of saving labor costs (Heywood et al. 2011). However, we must distinguish between the costs of temporary agency workers for the hiring companies and the wage of these employees. Many studies show that the wages of temporary agency workers are considerably below that of their permanently employed colleagues (Brown and Sessions 2005; Forde et al. 2008; Jahn 2010). Depending on the observation period, region and sector, Jahn (2010), Antoni and Jahn (2009) and Rudolph (2002) find a pay gap between temporary agency workers and core workers ranging from 15 to 30 % in Germany. In contrast, Forde et al. (2008) find a rather modest pay gap of roughly 10 % in Great Britain. However, as pointed out by Nollen (1996), even if wage gaps exist, the cost saving goal of hiring companies are often not met. This "disappointing experience appear[s] to occur in Europe as well as in the U.S." (Nollen 1996, p. 73).

The reason is that the client company does not directly pay the low wages. Instead, the client company pays a fee that includes the gross wage of the temporary worker and additional fees, depending on the contract, to the agency. These overhead fees are sometimes quite high, as pointed out by Houseman (2001). According to Ragnitz (2008), only two-thirds of the fee paid by the client company to the agency actually goes to the temporary worker; the rest goes toward the agency's overhead and profit. Another study on the German market find a difference of more than 50 % between the fee the client firm is charged and the average hourly wage of the temporary agency worker (Kvasnicka 2003). This means, in turn, that actual costs for a temporary agency worker, compared to a similar worker under a permanent contract, are at least the same or higher. This is confirmed in an empirical study by Kleinknecht et al. (2006, p. 176), which finds "evidence that flexible contracts lead to significant savings on firm's wage bill. This holds for people on truly temporary contracts and for self-employed ('free-lance') people. It does not, however, hold for people hired from manpower agencies." The findings of Kleinknecht et al. (2006) are in line with the survey results of Houseman (2001), where 62 % of the establishments respond that the hourly pay cost of temporary workers is generally higher, while 22 % judge them as about to be the same. Thus, it is important to note that using temporary agency work affects the competitiveness of firms through its effect on costs.

However, if saving labor costs is not the driving force behind the use of temporary agency work, it must have other features. Within the extensive literature on the positive and negative aspects of temporary agency work for the affected persons and the reasons to use it, we identify three discernible fundamental lines of argumentation and use them to derive our hypothesis on the relationship between temporary agency work and firm performance.[1]

4.2.1 *Temporary Employment and Increasing Labor Input Flexibility*

The first line of argumentation focuses on the flexibility of labor inputs through the use of temporary employees (Heywood et al. 2011). Theory suggests that the demand for flexible employment is driven by changes in product demand (Bentolila and Saint-Paul 1992). The greater the fluctuation in product demand, the greater the need for flexible labor input. This flexibility can be achieved in three different ways. In a completely flexible labor market, this would be achieved through the hiring and firing of labor. If external flexibility is reduced by high redundancy costs, the flexibility will to some extent be given by internal flexibility. However, external flexibility remains necessary and is achieved through temporary employment. Nunziata and Staffolani (2007) model this effect on the use of temporary work. Within their framework increasing termination costs will lead to the use of temporary employment in order to deal with product demand fluctuations.

Empirical evidence supports the theoretical findings. The use of temporary employment is greater in markets with stricter permanent employment protection (Booth et al. 2002a; Nunziata and Staffolani 2007; Shire et al. 2009). According to Autor (2003), a fifth of the increase in temporary agency work in the US is a result of growing employment protection. Heywood et al. (2011) find that establishments are more likely to use temporary employees when firms grant strong employment security to core workers. The results of Vidal and Tigges (2009) and Houseman (2001) show that the use of temporary employment is driven by variable product demand and the need to adjust labor input on short notice. This is also confirmed by the empirical analysis of Pfeifer (2005) for the German industry. Hence, using temporary agency work is beneficial for firms because it allows for quick reaction to changes in output demand by adjusting the cost of labor inputs while saving redundancy costs.

---

[1]Although this paper focuses on temporary agency work, which is defined as a triangular relationship between worker, leasing company and client (Burgess and Connell 2005), we do not explicitly distinguish between fixed-term contracts and temporary agency work in this literature review, because the discussed effects are rather similar for both forms of employment. This paper does also not discuss the institutional framework and its development in Germany. For more information, see Schmidt and Wuellerich (2011), Antoni and Jahn (2009), Mitlacher (2008) and Pfeifer (2005).

4.2.2 Temporary Employment and Screening

The second major discussion is about using temporary employment to screen potential new employees. Here, following the principal agent theory, the true quality of job applicants is unknown. Wang and Weiss (1998) provide a theoretical model where firms use temporary employment to screen new employees for a certain period. After the screening period, the more productive employees will be offered permanent employment directly by the firm. This increases productivity in two ways. First, during the probation period the employee has an incentive to increase his or her effort in order to gain an open end contract. These effects are confirmed by the findings of Engellandt and Riphahn (2005). Within their study they find that employees with temporary contracts have a greater probability to work unpaid overtime compared to those employees with open end contracts. Second, giving open end contracts only to the more productive employees after the probation period will increase the productivity in the long run. Further empirical evidence for the screening argument is found by Beckmann and Kuhn (2012), Buddelmeyer and Wooden (2011), Addison and Surfield (2009) and Booth et al. (2002b).

However, if firm policy or recent events prove that fixed-term contracts or temporary agency work is not used to screen for the productive workers but rather are substitutes for permanent contracts, the positive incentives of screening will fail to appear (George 2003). Such substitution could discourage the remaining core workers and the resulting "low levels of job satisfaction and morale may exert an adverse influence on productivity levels."(Brown and Sessions 2005, p. 311). However, this effect is conditional "upon the proportion of temporary workers and upon permanent workers' assumptions concerning the reasons for hiring temporary workers" (DeCuyper et al. 2008, p. 39). Thus, using too many temporary agency worker will negatively effect the productivity of all workers and, subsequently, decrease firm competitiveness via decreased firm productivity and vice versa.

4.2.3 Temporary Employment and Human Capital

Finally, the last effect through which temporary agency work affects firm performance is the relationship between human capital and productivity. The latter depends on firm-specific human capital, established and maintained through on the job training (Zwick 2006). As pointed out by Nollen (1996), temporary agency worker receive less training since it is costly and due to the short-term nature of agency work, such an investment would not pay off: "Therefore, temporary employment is adverse to human capital development contributed by either staffing company, worksite employer, or direct-hire employer" (Nollen 1996, p. 575). Such considerations are supported by empirical findings. In the study of Booth et al. (2002b), temporary employees have up to a 20 % lower probability of receiving training, as well as significantly fewer training days than permanent workers when

Table 4.1 Effect of temporary agency work on competitiveness via three main mechanisms

	Flexibility	Screening/ motivation	Human capital
Low share of temporary agency workers	+	+	−
High share of temporary agency workers	+	−	−

they do receive training. This is also supported by the findings of Albert et al. (2005) and by various studies for the German market (Mitlacher 2008). However, the study by Zwick (2006) revealed the positive relationship between training and firm productivity. Hence, an increasing number of temporary agency workers should have a negative effect on the firm's competitiveness.

4.2.4 Temporary Employment and Firm Performance

In summary, temporary agency work affects firm competitiveness through different mechanisms and, as shown in Table 4.1, the overall effect depends on the share of temporary workers on firms' workforce. Hence, the use of temporary agency workers has a positive effect since it allows for greater flexibility and it allows firms to screen potential new employees. On the other hand, using temporary agency workers will decrease firms' productivity via lower firm specific human capital. Further, an ever increasing share of temporary agency workers reduces internal motivation and also decreases productivity. Essentially firms face a trade-off between increased flexibility and the possibility to screen new employees on the one hand, with less firm specific human capital and less motivated employees on the other. To what extent the positive or negative effects ultimately prevail depends on the share of temporary agency workers. We therefore expect to find a nonlinear, perhaps inverse U-shaped relationship between firm competitiveness and the extent that temporary agency workers are used by the firms.

4.3 Related Studies

As shown above, a large and growing body of the literature is devoted to the relationship between temporary agency work, labor market performance and the situation of temporary employees. There is, however, only limited research on the effect of temporary agency work on firm performance.

The first who accounted for the effect of temporary agency work on firm performance was Arvanitis (2005). Using data on 1,382 Swiss firms across all sectors, he evaluates the effect of various forms of labor flexibility on the performance and the innovative activity of the firms. One instrument controlled for is temporary agency work. It is included in the analysis as a dummy variable that takes the value of one if companies reported that temporary agency work is important for them. The output variable is sales per capita, which approximates labor productivity. Using OLS, the results indicate that temporary agency work has no significant effect on the output variable sales per capita. The second is Kleinknecht et al. (2006), who study 590 Dutch firms from different sectors for the years 1992–1994 using an OLS approach to analyze the effect of temporary agency workers on sales growth and employment growth. The explanatory variable measuring the input of temporary workers is the percentage of hours worked by temporary agency workers on total hours worked. They also do not find a positive effect on their output variable. However, they find a weak, but negative, relationship between the use of temporary agency workers and sales growth among non-innovators, while the effect on employment growth is insignificant. According to Kleinknecht et al. (2006), this suggests that labor productivity might be negatively affected by hired labor from manpower agencies.

The paper of Bryson (2007) uses data from approximately 1,500 British companies to measure the potential effect of temporary agency work on firm performance. Using OLS on the endogenous variables logged sales per employee and logged gross value added per worker, temporary agency work is modeled by three dummy variables that take the value of one if a company has none, 1–4 % or 5 or more percent of temporary workers on total workforce, respectively. The results indicate that there is no significant effect of the use of temporary worker on firm's performance.

For Germany, Beckmann and Kuhn (2009) were the first to analyze the effect of temporary agency work on firm performance. They use a large data set of German establishments, the IAB panel of the Institute of Employment Research with almost 12,000 companies, but only 25,000 observations for the 2000–2005 period. Hence, the average number of observations per firm is 2.1. They model a Cobb-Douglas production function where logged sales is the output variable, explained by various control variables and two variable categories that cover temporary workers. First, the share of temporary workers on total workforce and its quadratic term is included. Second, four dummy variables are defined that take the value of one if a company employs no temporary workers, 1–10 %, 11–30 % or more than 30 % of temporary workers on total workforce. Using OLS, as well as a fixed effect and a random effect models, they find an inverse U-shaped relationship between changes in sales and the share of temporary workers on total workforce. According to this result, the share of temporary agency workers should not exceed 10–15 % in total employment.

In a further study, again using the IAB data, Beckmann and Kuhn (2012) focus on analyzing the effect of a flexibility versus a screening strategy on firm performance. To this end, they make use of the wave of 2003, which asked for the reasons of using temporary agency work. Firm performance is measured by logged value added, logged sales and logged sales per capita. Modeling both strategies with dummy variables and applying the Black-Lynch approach, they find that establishments using the screening strategy outperform those that apply the flexibility strategy, regardless of the dependent variables.

Finally, Hirsch and Mueller (2012), investigate the effect of temporary agency work on firm performance, using the same data set as (Beckmann and Kuhn 2009), but only for the 2003–2009 period. As in Beckmann and Kuhn (2009), the analysis is based on a Cobb-Douglas function and various controls, with the difference that the dependent variable is logged gross value added. The effect of temporary agency work is modeled by 9 dummy variables as well as the percentage of temporary employees in the workforce and its squared term. Like Beckmann and Kuhn (2009), they account for the problem of time-invariant unobserved plant heterogeneity by applying a fixed effect estimator. In addition, they make use of the system GMM approach in order to address potential endogeneity problems. The authors find a significant hump-shaped relationship between the extent of the use of temporary agency workers and firm productivity. Their preferred system GMM specification points at a maximum productivity effect at a share of 11.3% of temporary agency workers in total workforce.

This study contributes to the existing literature mainly in two ways: it uses a large data set with more than 26,000 firms and 101,000 observations that observe the use of temporary agency work over the course of a year. This is an advantage over the previous German studies, which used date data instead of yearly data on the use of temporary agency work. More precisely, in the questionnaire of the IAB it is asked whether any temporary agency workers were being used on June 30 of that year.[2]

Due to the nature of temporary agency work, it might very well be that firms report to have no agency workers on that June 30th, but that they used non, a few or many either before or after the 30th of June.[3] At the same time, sales or value added refer to the entire year in the IAB panel. Thus, we see at least the possibility that some firms are included in the analysis as non-users, producing given sales, even though they might have actually used temporary agency workers.[4] This might have an effect on the magnitude and the significance of coefficients. In contrast, the data

[2]The questionnaire can be downloaded for each year. See http://fdz.iab.de/en/FDZ_Establishment_Data/IAB_Establishment_Panel/IAB_Establishment_Panel_Working_Tools.aspx. Moreover, Städele and Müller (2006) provide a detailed description for each variable up to 2005.

[3]Employment duration for more than 50 % of all temporary agency workers is less than 3 months (Schmidt and Wuellerich 2011).

[4]Some descriptive statistics indicate that this observation problem exists and that there is a difference between date data and annual data. According to Hirsch and Mueller (2012), about 24.4 % of all plants in their sample (1,556 out of 6,375) have used temporary agency at least once in the observation period (2003–2009). In our dataset, we find that roughly 63 % of all firms in the sample used temporary agency work at least once. Now, these shares are not easy to compare: Firstly, the observation unit in the IAB establishment panel is an establishment, while it is a company in our data set. Secondly, the observation periods differ, as Hirsch and Mueller (2012) analyze the 2003–2009 period, while this study analyzes the 1999–2006 period. Though, using an earlier period should rather have the effect that the share in our data set is lower, given the raising number of temporary agency workers since 2000. Eventually, the explanation for the difference might simply be the fact that the IAB questionnaire specifically asked for the number of temporary agency workers at the 30th of June.

set used in this study contains spending on temporary agency work over the course of the year, avoiding a potential bias. Another advantage of this study is the applied dependent variable – unit labor costs – which is a measure for competitiveness. By using this variable, the analysis not only takes into account potential productivity effects of temporary agency work, but also potential cost effects. If there are positive, or, as some studies indicate, actually negative cost effects of temporary agency work (Houseman 2001; Kleinknecht et al. 2006; Kvasnicka 2003; Nollen 1996), they are accounted for in the analysis.

4.4 Data

This study uses a newly constructed data set of German Manufacturing enterprises. It contains data from the German Cost Structure Census *(Kostenstrukturerhebung)*, the German Production Census *(Produktionserhebung)* and the Monthly Reports of German Manufacturing enterprises *(Monatsbericht)*.[5] Each data set was gathered and complied by the Federal Statistical Office and the statistical offices of the states *(Statistisches Bundesamt, Statistische Landesämter)*, with firms legally obliged to provide data.

The most important data set for this analysis is that of the Cost Structure Census (CSC). According to the law, all firms with more than 500 employees are always part of the Census. Smaller firms with 20–500 employees are included in the surveys as random subsamples that are designed to be representative for each sector. These subsamples are held constant for 4 years.[6] Thus, the strength of the data sets is their coverage and reliability since they contain representative data for each German manufacturing sector. The data set contains information on several input categories, such as expenditures for material inputs, wages and benefits, costs for temporary agency workers, depreciation, etc.[7] The Production Census (PC) contains information on the good produced, based on the nine-digit product classification system *(Güterverzeichnis für Produktionsstatistiken)* of the Federal Statistical Office. Just as with the CSC, all firms are legally obliged to provide data. Unlike the CSC, the PC is a total survey with cut-off limits. Hence, it contains all

[5]The data are confidential and can only be used by remote execution. However, they are not exclusive. For more information see Zuehlke et al. (2004) and http://www.forschungsdatenzentrum.de/en/index.asp.

[6]The subsamples are compiled in 1999 and 2003.

[7]For more information about the Cost Structure Census surveys in Germany, see Fritsch et al. (2004).

German manufacturing firms with more than 20 employees.[8] It provides information about the number and value of products produced by companies according to the nine-digit product classification system. We use it to identify single- and multi-product firms. Like the PC, the Monthly Reports (MR) is a total survey with a cut-off limit. It contains information on domestic sales and foreign sales (differentiated by Euro and non-Euro Area) as well as orders for all German manufacturing firms with more than 20 employees. This data set allows us to measure the export intensity of firms. We use the data for the 1999–2006 period. Plant and firm level data are merged using a common identifier.

By doing this, our data set is reduced to those firms that have a match in the CSC. Moreover, before starting the analysis we conduct some basic data preparation, namely looking for missing values or typing errors as well as implausible large differences in sales between the CSC and the MR. Thus, although the data set used covers 26,725 firms and contains 101,433 observations, we do not regard it as representative for the entire German manufacturing sector. This newly constructed data set contains information identifying the company, year, industry classification, number of employees, sales, commission, self-constructed assets, raw materials at the begin and end of the period as well as new raw materials, energy, trading goods, gross wage costs, statutory social costs, other social costs, costs for temporary workers, costs for performed contract work, cost of repairs, costs for long-term rental units, other costs, insurance, depreciation, the establishment profile, legal form, number of products, etc. However, it does not include information about socio-economic characteristics of workers or groups of employees, the worker turnover rate, unionization or the like. For a more detailed description of the underlying individual data sets and the information contained therein, we refer to Wagner (2000, 2010b) and Fritsch et al. (2004).

Given the data, the dependent variable that measures competitiveness is the logarithm of unit labor costs (ULC). It is a direct and widely used measure of competitiveness (Alesina and Perotti 1997; Felipe 2007; van Ark et al. 2005).[9] It is constructed by dividing the cost of labor, including all benefits, by real value added, or formally as $ULC = w_n L/(VA_n/P)$, with the numerator capturing labor costs and the denominator the real value added. This can easily be transformed into $ULC = w_n/((VA_n/P)/L)$ and $ULC = w_n/(Q/L)$ by substituting real value added

[8]Starting in 2010 the cut-off limits were increased to 50 employees in order to reduce bureaucratic burdens for smaller firms. However, this does not affect our analysis since we use data from before 2010.

[9]ULC as indicator for competitiveness is, for instance, provided and used by the OECD or the Bureau of Labor Statistics. See: http://stats.oecd.org/mei/default.asp?rev=3, http://www.bls.gov/news.release/prod4.t03.htm

by quantities (Felipe 2007). Hence, ULC is driven by wages as well as by labor productivity.[10] Thus, ULC is a superior competitiveness measure compared to labor productivity, since, as pointed out by van Ark et al. (2005, p. 2), "competitiveness is not only determined by productivity, but also by the cost of inputs in the production process. Indeed, a well-known measure of international competitiveness combines labour cost and productivity into a single measure of labour cost per unit output."[11]

Using ULC also solves a data issue. In order to measure, say, labor productivity, appropriately, one needs working hours of temporary agency workers and core workers. Using the number of heads over the year is misleading, as it is unclear how long a temporary agency worker actually worked in a firm. This problem could, of course, be overcome either by making use of working hours or by yearly full time equivalence. Yet, so far there is no data set for Germany that gives working hours for temporary agency workers in client firms, nor full time equivalents. Our data set, however, is the only German firm level data set where data on spending on temporary agency workers for the entire year is available. Thus, given the data constrains with respect to temporary agency work, ULC as a common competitive measure is applicable and allows us, other than labor productivity, to appropriately account for the impact of agency workers in producing the output.

Given the data set and according to the definition of ULC,[12] we measure the share of temporary agency workers on total firm employment, by dividing the costs for temporary agency workers with the sum of labor costs for permanent employees and costs for temporary agency workers *(Share)*. Since we expect the relationship between a firm's competitiveness and the share of temporary agency workers on the total workforce to be nonlinear, we also used the squared Share variable *(Share2)*. Table 4.2 contains the descriptive statistics for the Share variable at the industry level.

Looking at column three, we see that the mean share of costs of temporary employees on total labor cost is rather low, ranging from 0.4 to 4.7 % for the entire data set. The variation, however, is quite large. Looking just at the 99 percentiles in each industry we see a range from 8.8 % to 35 %. The high variation and the low means are caused by two things. First, about 10,000 firms never

---

[10]For international comparisons, the purchasing power parity and exchange rates must also be considered. See for an introduction see van Ark et al. (2005).

[11]We are aware of the critics and limitations of ULC. First, changes in the second input category, capital, are not explicitly taken into account. Second, the way ULC is defined it can also be interpreted as a measure of the share of labor income on output (Felipe 2007). We address these issues by considering the capital intensity of production as an explanatory variable in the estimation.

[12]Given this data set, we construct ULC by using gross value added deflated by the producer price index at a two digit industry classification and the sum of all labor costs. The latter include wages, social security expenditures, provisions for firm pensions etc. Moreover, we also include the costs of temporary agency workers in the denominator.

Table 4.2 Share per industry

	Entire data set					Only observations using TAW				
WZ	Mean	p1	p99	sd	N	Mean	p1	p99	sd	N
15	0.0199	0.0000	0.2742	0.0574	12,125	0.0533	0.0003	0.4422	0.0839	4,528
16	0.0290			0.0549	73	0.0543			0.0656	39
17	0.0076	0.0000	0.1143	0.0268	3,721	0.0253	0.0001	0.1918	0.0440	1,118
18	0.0041	0.0000	0.0578	0.0406	1,107	0.0382	0.0002	0.7106	0.1190	119
19	0.0101	0.0000	0.1846	0.0304	789	0.0370	0.0003	0.2527	0.0489	215
20	0.0151	0.0000	0.1627	0.0344	2,809	0.0358	0.0002	0.2356	0.0455	1,184
21	0.0111	0.0000	0.1162	0.0227	2,709	0.0223	0.0002	0.1260	0.0280	1,344
22	0.0075	0.0000	0.1438	0.0333	6,264	0.0282	0.0001	0.3030	0.0600	1,663
23	0.0102	0.0000	0.0953	0.0217	204	0.0209	0.0002	0.1517	0.0272	100
24	0.0161	0.0000	0.1546	0.0342	5,986	0.0283	0.0002	0.2063	0.0413	3,413
25	0.0210	0.0000	0.1803	0.0409	5,981	0.0369	0.0002	0.2318	0.0485	3,405
26	0.0169	0.0000	0.2014	0.0451	5,252	0.0364	0.0003	0.2881	0.0606	2,441
27	0.0220	0.0000	0.2013	0.0415	3,966	0.0370	0.0001	0.2249	0.0484	2,355
28	0.0310	0.0000	0.3325	0.0655	11,966	0.0540	0.0003	0.4154	0.0789	6,875
29	0.0237	0.0000	0.2281	0.0491	15,865	0.0401	0.0002	0.2803	0.0586	9,362
30	0.0212	0.0000	0.2688	0.0554	859	0.0498	0.0005	0.3693	0.0761	366
31	0.0228	0.0000	0.2643	0.0500	5,672	0.0423	0.0002	0.2995	0.0617	3,06
32	0.0195	0.0000	0.2135	0.0431	1,83	0.0397	0.0003	0.2860	0.0547	897
33	0.0126	0.0000	0.1861	0.0359	3,976	0.0325	0.0001	0.2841	0.0518	1,54
34	0.0358	0.0000	0.2892	0.0621	3,76	0.0532	0.0004	0.3257	0.0693	2,533
35	0.0465	0.0000	0.3501	0.0761	1,577	0.0715	0.0005	0.3875	0.0844	1,025
36	0.0139	0.0000	0.1660	0.0362	4,942	0.0351	0.0002	0.2261	0.0506	1,957

Notes: Due to private policy of the Research Data Centers, some percentiles are not publishable due to the small number of cases in the respective subgroups. Sector number according to the statistical classification of economic activities of NACE Rev. 1.1.: 15: Manufacture of food products and beverages; 16: Manufacture of tobacco products; 17: Manufacture of textiles; 18: Manufacture of wearing apparel; dressing and dyeing of fur; 19: Tanning and dressing of leather; manufacture of luggage, handbags, saddlery, harness and footwear; 20: Manufacture of wood and of products of wood and cork, except furniture; manufacture of articles of straw and plaiting materials; 21: Manufacture of paper and paper products; 22: Publishing, printing and reproduction of recorded media; 23: Manufacture of coke, refined petroleum products and nuclear fuel; 24: Manufacture of chemicals and chemical products; 25: Manufacture of rubber and plastics products; 26: Manufacture of other non-metallic mineral products; 27: Manufacture of basic metals; 28: Manufacture of fabricated metal products, except machinery and equipment; 29: Manufacture of machinery and equipment n.e.c.; 30: Manufacture of office, accounting and computing machinery; 31: Manufacture of electrical machinery and apparatus n.e.c.; 32: Manufacture of radio, television and communication equipment and apparatus; 33: Manufacture of medical, precision and optical instruments, watches and clocks; 34: Manufacture of motor vehicles, trailers and semi-trailers; 35: Manufacture of other transport equipment; 36: Manufacture of furniture; manufacturing n.e.c used temporary agency workers at all during the period under observation. This is a share of about 37 %. Second, the firms that used temporary agency workers often only used it moderately. However, as presented in column 8–12, showing the descriptive statistics for all observations where temporary agency worker are used, the mean ranges from 2.1 to 7.2 %, while the 99 percentile reaches 71 %. Thus, a considerable number of firms rented labor extensively. The remaining explanatory variables are size of a company (Size) measured by the number of employees in order to capture scale effects and the number of products *(NoProducts)* to take into account economies of scope or specialization effects. Moreover, the variable average labor costs *(AvageLaborCosts)* is included for two reasons: First, it captures effects on wages due to firm policy, like for example firm wages above industry average wages, which directly affects ULC. Second, this variable is supposed to cover some of the effect of human capital, since a higher level of human capital goes in line with higher average labor costs. The share of outsourced activities like repair and costs for contract work performed by other companies on gross value added (External) is also included, because a higher level of outsourcing activities reduces unit labor costs. Another important variable is the capital intensity of production *(CapitalIntensity)* calculated as a quotient of capital stocks[13] and the number of employees, since higher capital intensity should increase labor productivity leading to lower unit labor costs. We also control for the material intensity of production as share of material and energy costs on sales *(IntermediateIntensity)*, because a higher material intensity should be related to higher labor productivity, since it indicates that a firm is located at the upper end of the value chain. Finally, we include the export intensity as a share of foreign sales on total sales *(ExportIntensity)* to take into account productivity effects resulting from export activity. We apply the logarithm of these variables in the analysis.

Further, we make use of dummy variables for the years *(YearDummies)* and the industries*(IndustryDummies)* as well as dummy variables for the establishment profile *(EstablishmentProfile)*. Regarding establishment profile, the data distinguishes between single plant firms, multi plant firms and multi country firms. Finally, the inverse Mills ratio *(InversMillsRatio)* is calculated and used as an explanatory variable to account for the selection bias. The descriptive statistics for all variables are shown in Table 4.3.

[13]The capital stock is not given in the data. It is approximated by a program recently published by Wagner (2010a).

Table 4.3 Descriptive statistics

Variable		Mean	Std. Dev.	Observations
ULC	Overall	0.3146	0.1410	N = 101433
	Between		0.1395	n = 26725
	Within		0.0400	T-bar = 379.543
Share	Overall	0.0203	0.0490	N = 101433
	Between		0.0457	n = 26725
	Within		0.0225	T-bar = 379.543
Size	Overall	2767956.00	2169083.00	N = 101433
	Between		1709377.00	n = 26725
	Within		1419057.00	T-bar = 379.543
NoProducts	Overall	3848126.00	8689191.00	N = 101433
	Between		8083096.00	n = 26725
	Within		1716048.00	T-bar = 379.543
AvageLaborCosts	Overall	36886.71	12934.56	N = 101433
	Between		12754.37	n = 26725
	Within		3562866.00	T-bar = 379.543
External	Overall	0.0533	0.0701	N = 101433
	Between		0.0705	n = 26725
	Within		0.0271	T-bar = 379.543
CapitalIntensity	Overall	92131.96	135051.40	N = 101433
	Between		126639.20	n = 26725
	Within		45188.34	T-bar = 379.543
IntermediateIntensity	Overall	0.4130	0.2088	N = 101433
	Between		0.1881	n = 26725
	Within		0.0988	T-bar = 379.543
ExportIntensity	Overall	0.2238	0.2500	N = 101433
	Between		0.2393	n = 26725
	Within		0.0528	T-bar = 379.543
EstablishmentProfile1	Overall	0.8460	0.3609	N = 101433
	Between		0.3667	n = 26725
	Within		0.0056	T-bar = 379.543
EstablishmentProfile2	Overall	0.0526	0.2233	N = 101433
	Between		0.2321	n = 26725
	Within		0.0390	T-bar = 379.543
EstablishmentProfile3	Overall	0.1014	0.3018	N = 101433
	Between		0.3007	n = 26725
	Within		0.0390	T-bar = 379.543
LegalForm1	Overall	0.3703	0.4829	N = 101433
	Between		0.4739	n = 26725
	Within		0.0980	T-bar = 379.543

(continued)

Table 4.3 (continued)

Variable		Mean	Std. Dev.	Observations
LegalForm2	Overall	0.6259	0.4839	N = 101433
	Between		0.4752	n = 26725
	Within		0.0963	T-bar = 379.543
LegalForm3	Overall	0.0038	0.0615	N = 101433
	Between		0.0565	n = 26725
	Within		0.0213	T-bar = 379.543

4.5 Empirical Investigation

To analyze the relationship between the extent of using temporary agency work and ULC, we proceed in three steps. First, we present the empirical strategy and the applied methods. Second, we present and discuss the estimation results. Finally, the last subsection presents the results of robustness checks.

4.5.1 Methods and Empirical Strategy

As noted before, about 63 % of all companies in the data set have used temporary agency workers at least once. It follows that the analysis is subject to a self-selection problem since some firms have never used temporary agency work. If this selection problem is not taken into account, there is a risk of estimating biased or inconsistent estimators and to exaggerate or underestimate the effect of temporary agency work. Therefore, our analysis starts with the estimation of a probit selection equation, where the dependent variable is a binary variable that takes the value of one if a firm uses temporary agency work in given year and zero otherwise.[14] Given the estimates we calculate the inverse Mills ratio based on the selection model as proposed by Heckmann (1979). For details of this approach see Briggs (2004). This ratio is then included in subsequent estimations as an additional variable to control for the possible selection effect. As an exclusion restriction we use three dummy variables for the legal form *(LegalForm)* of the companies. The data distinguishes between firms with personally liable owners, capital companies and state or local entity owned firms. The idea behind this is the following: We expect firms with a different legal status to have different incentives in making use of temporary agency workers. First, firms in which the owner is present and also personally liable, so called family firms, are supposed to have a closer relationship with their workforce. This might

[14]We do not make use of all available variables in the selection equation because variables in the selection model and in the regression models should not be identical in order to avoid multicollinearity between the inverse Mills ratio and the other exogenous variables (Briggs 2004; Puhani 2000).

lead to a lower incentive to make use of temporary agency work compared to capital companies. Moreover, firms that are owned, at least partly, by a state or local entity may have a lower probability to make use of temporary agency work because it is not desirable for political reasons (see Bogetoft and Hougaard (2003) on rational inefficiencies). Another requirement for a valid exclusion restriction is exogeneity. Potential endogeneity could result from reversed causality or simultaneity. Since the legal status of a firm is rather stable over time, reverse causality and simultaneity can be excluded as a reason for endogeneity of our exclusion restriction. Furthermore, there are no economic reasons why unit labor costs should have any impact on the decision regarding the legal status of a firm. Another reason for endogneity could be measurement errors. However, it should be very unlikely that legal status is affected by measurement errors. Moreover, VIFs after OLS Regression indicate that there is no problem of multicollinearity between the inverse Mills ratio and the explanatory variables.[15] Hence our model is well identified.

To test the hypothesis that the relationship between the competitiveness of firms and the extent that temporary agency workers are used by firms is U-shaped, we estimate of the following equation:

$$log(ULC_{it}) = \beta_1 Share_{it} + \beta_2 Share2_{it} + \gamma_k log(x_{kit}) + \theta_m D_{mit} + \delta Mills_{it} + v_i + u_{it}$$

with $i = 1, \ldots, N, t = 1, \ldots, T, Share = log(1+Share)$ and $Share2 = 0.5 * Share^2$. $Share_{it}$ is the quotient of expenses for temporary agency worker and total labor costs. X_{kit} denotes all continuous control variables, D_{mit} indicates all dummy variables including year dummies, except the LegalForm dummies, which are used in the selection equation only and $Mills_{it}$ captures the self-selection into the use of temporary workers via inverse Mills ratio. Finally with v_i denotes a firm specific fixed effect and u_{it} is the error term capturing unsystematic influences of ULC.

The estimation strategy for measuring the effect of temporary agency work on the competitiveness of firms on behalf of this estimation equation is as follows: First, we estimate an OLS regression model including all control variables to gain an impression of the relationship between the variables of interest: *Share*, *Share2* (Share squared) and ULC. Then, we estimate a fixed effect regression in order to control for firm specific effects. The estimation is conducted taking into account all control variables, as described above. Since there is variation over time, the dummy variables are also included.[16]

---

[15]The table with the results for the VIFs is available on request from the authors. To check the robustness of our results regarding a changing exclusion restriction, we estimate three alternative exclusion restrictions. First a dummy that takes the value of one if at least one owner is working in the firm; second we use a combination of legal status dummies and the dummy variable taking value of one if at least one owner is working in the firm and third we estimate the model without any exclusion restriction only identifying it via nonlinearity. Our results of the second stage regressions are not affected by changes in the exclusion restriction: the respective results are available on request from the authors.

[16]The fixed effect model was also estimated without dummy variables. We do not report the results, since the level of the coefficients changes minimally, while signs and significances do not change.

However, fixed effect models do not take into account the possible endogeneity of regressors or dynamic effects. Therefore, we also make use of dynamic panel data models. A natural choice is the difference GMM estimator proposed by Arellano and Bond (1991). Here, the estimation equation is transformed into first differences. In order to account for the dynamic effects, the (differenced) lagged dependent variable is included as an additional explanatory variable. Since it is endogenous by nature, it is instrumented with its own values of lag order two and higher.

One critical point of the difference GMM estimator, as well as of the fixed effect estimator, is the elimination of level information by subtracting means over time or first differences. Using the level information could improve estimations. Therefore we apply the estimator proposed by Arellano and Bover (1995) and Blundell and Bond (1998), called system GMM.[17] System GMM estimates a model in first differences and one in levels simultaneously using additional moment conditions compared to difference GMM. Following Blundell and Bond (1998), the lagged values of the variables are used as instruments for the differenced variables in the difference model, while in the level model lagged differences are used as instruments for the variables in levels. For all specifications the p-values of the Hansen test of overidentifying restrictions are reported. It is also important to test for first order autocorrelation of the error terms in levels. This is done by a test for second order autocorrelation of first differences.

The actual analysis, based on system GMM, involves three estimates. First, a model is estimated where the potential endogeneity of regressors is ignored. In the second GMM estimate we additionally assume that the Share variables are not strictly exogenous, but predetermined. This means they are correlated with past error terms but not with current ones. Third, the Share variables are assumed to be endogenous, meaning that they are assumed to be correlated with past as well as current error terms.

4.5.2 Estimation Results of Static and Dynamic Panel Data Models

The analysis starts by estimating a selection equation to deal with potential self-selection. The first column in Table 4.4 contains the outcome of the applied probit model. As noted before, these estimates are used to calculate the inverse Mills ratio, which is then included as an additional control variable in all subsequent estimations to take into account the selection problem. The actual analysis of the

[17]Following Roodman (2009b), we reduce the number of instruments by collapsing them because too many instruments could lead to a bias in estimates. Without collapsing, the number of instruments increases by 2.5 times from 65 to 163. This heavily affects the Hansen test of exogeneity of instruments. However, the estimated coefficients are minimally affected. Although the tables are omitted from this paper, the results are available upon request from the authors.

Table 4.4 Estimation results of static and dynamic panel data models with controlling for the selection effect via the inverse Mills ratio

	Probit	OLS	Fixed Effect	Sys GMM (1)	Sys GMM (2)	Sys GMM (3)
Endogenous variable	TAW dummy	ULC	ULC	ULC	ULC	ULC
Lag one of ULC				0.499***	0.495***	0.500***
				(0.0187)	(0.0187)	(0.0188)
Share		−0.107***	−0.114***	−0.0835***	−0.122***	−0.0471
		(0.0114)	(0.0137)	(0.0124)	(0.0225)	(0.0479)
Share2		0.703***	1.091***	0.610***	0.988***	−0.0599
		(0.0922)	(0.105)	(0.115)	(0.205)	(0.413)
Size	0.300213***	−0.000667**	0.0247***	−0.000690**	−0.000609*	−0.000731**
	(0.0051687)	(0.000296)	(0.00190)	(0.000316)	(0.000323)	(0.000339)
NoProducts	−0.0343466***	0.00561***	−4.05e-05	0.00171***	0.00173***	0.00162***
	(0.005839)	(0.000304)	(0.000869)	(0.000332)	(0.000336)	(0.000337)
AvageLaborCosts	0.6916828***	−0.00461***	0.0632***	0.00729***	0.00737***	0.00722***
	(0.0140922)	(0.000922)	(0.00214)	(0.000972)	(0.000985)	(0.000981)
External	1.077105***	−0.335***	−0.142***	−0.178***	−0.178***	−0.178***
	(0.0794678)	(0.00631)	(0.00932)	(0.00771)	(0.00775)	(0.00774)
CapitalIntensity	0.0184401***	−0.0184***	−0.00520***	−0.00937***	−0.00943***	−0.00935***
	(0.0041781)	(0.000281)	(0.000475)	(0.000441)	(0.000442)	(0.000439)
IntermediateIntensity	0.194081***	−0.0915***	−0.0321***	−0.0455***	−0.0457***	−0.0455***
	(0.0082465)	(0.000853)	(0.00156)	(0.00172)	(0.00172)	(0.00171)
ExportIntensity	0.1047487***	−0.0513***	−0.0482***	−0.0327***	−0.0328***	−0.0329***
	(0.0263184)	(0.00148)	(0.00494)	(0.00192)	(0.00193)	(0.00195)
InversMillsRatio		−0.000123	−0.0644***	0.00269	0.00243	0.00258
		(0.00238)	(0.00502)	(0.00239)	(0.00241)	(0.00239)
EstablishmentProfile2	−0.1273013***	0.0106***	0.0362***	0.00627***	0.00627***	0.00625***
	(0.0195473)	(0.00105)	(0.00961)	(0.00119)	(0.00120)	(0.00118)

EstablishmentProfile3	0.0654878***	−0.00768***	0.0374***	−0.00420***	−0.00425***	−0.00405***
	(0.0160955)	(0.000849)	(0.00971)	(0.000931)	(0.000937)	(0.000936)
LegalForm2	0.0141533					
	(0.0088645)					
LegalForm3	−0.3172721***					
	(0.0704008)					
Year dummies	Yes	Yes	Yes	Yes	Yes	Yes
Industry dummies	Yes	Yes	Yes	Yes	Yes	Yes
Constant	−8.999184***	0.402***	−0.358***	0.0996***	0.100***	0.100***
	(0.1368693)	(0.0103)	(0.0291)	(0.0139)	(0.0140)	(0.0139)
(Pseudo) R2	0.1486	0.509	0.185			
Number of ID			26,725	23,514	23,514	23,514
Observations	101,433	101,433	101,433	73,173	73,173	73,173
No. of instruments				47	61	59
Wald chi2	15905.41			61200.72	59760.76	60529.46
AR(2) test p-value				0.302	0.299	0.323
Hansen test p-value				0.001	0.001	0.001
Optimal share		16.44 %	11.01 %	14.67 %	13.14 %	–

Robust standard errors in parentheses; Sys. GMM: Share variables treated as (1) exogenous, (2) predetermined, (3) endogenous
* p<0.1; ** p<0.05; *** p<0.01

relationship between ULC and the use of temporary agency work begins with an OLS model followed by a fixed effects model. The results of these estimates are given in column two and three. Column four presents the system GMM model treating all explanatory variables as exogenous, except the lagged dependent one, which is endogenous by the nature of the model. In contrast, both Share variables are treated as predetermined in the system GMM model in column five. These are treated this way in order to check whether previous results are affected by potential endogeneity due to correlation with past error terms. Column six provides the results for the system GMM model where both Share variables are treated as endogenous.

Starting with the OLS model, we find a negative and significant coefficient for the variable Share and a significant positive coefficient for the Share2 variable. Controlling for firm specific fixed effects leads to higher values for the coefficients of both Share variables, but the signs and significances are not affected. The same is true for the first and the second system GMM estimates. In the last system GMM model the relationship between the use of temporary agency work and unit labor costs seems to be negative. But, however, the relative high standard errors for both coefficients indicate that they might be affected by the weak instrument problem. This problem arises if the lagged values with order of two or higher are only weakly related to the first difference and are therefore a weak instrument. Hence, the results of the first five columns show that an increase of the Share variable decreases ULC and, therefore, increases firm competitiveness. The positive sign of the coefficient of the squared Share variable shows on the other hand, that this is not a linear relationship, but that the rising competitiveness turned into a declining one, if the share of temporary agency worker increases too much. Hence, our hypothesis of a nonlinear relationship between the ULC and the extent to which temporary agency work is used by the firms is confirmed in all models, except the one model where both Share variables are assumed to be endogenous.

With respect to the control variables, the following is found: The coefficient for firm size is negative in all models, except in the fixed effects model, and significant in all models, which indicates that unit labor costs decreases with firm size.[18] The coefficient of the variable number of products is always positive except in the fixed effects model. For the variable average labor costs we find a positive and significant coefficient in all models, except in the OLS model. The coefficients of the variables external, capital intensity, intermediate intensity and export intensity have the expected negative sign and are significant in all models. Additionally, the coefficient of the inverse Mills ratio is negative and significant only in the fixed effects model. In the OLS as well as in all system GMM models the coefficient

[18]The literature also discusses whether the relationship between firm size and firm performance is nonlinear. Schiersch (2013), for example, finds a U-shaped relationship between technical efficiency and firm size in the case of the German mechanical engineering industry. We therefore test if this relationship can also be found between ULC and firm size, and whether it has any influence on the relationship between the use of temporary agency workers and ULC. The coefficients of Share and Share2 are not affected if we include a squared firm size term. Although not presented here, results are available upon request from the authors.

of the inverse mills ratio is not significant. Hence, when using within and between variations, the control variables included in our regression model capture most of the potential selection effect, if there is any. With respect to the estimation quality note that, on the one hand, the test for autocorrelation of the error terms in levels in all system GMM specifications performs well. On the other hand, the null hypothesis of the Hansen test of over-identifying restrictions is rejected for all system GMM estimations. The reasons for the rejection of the null hypothesis are heterogeneities in the relationship between unit labor costs and some explanatory variables.[19]

To sum up, the results of most models reported in Table 4.4 support our hypothesis of a nonlinear, U-shaped (inverse) relationship between the unit labor costs (competiveness) and the extent that temporary agency workers are used by firms. Only in the system GMM model in which both Share variables are modeled as being endogenous, our hypothesis finds no support.

Given the coefficients for the Share variable and its squared form, we can calculate an optimal share of temporary agency workers, ceteris paribus. However, one should be careful interpreting the results, because the measure for the intensity of using temporary agency workers is calculated as the share of temporary agency work on total spending for labor. Then, the optimal share, based on the results of the OLS model, is about 16 %. However, OLS is affected by a fixed effects bias. When controlling for firm specific effects by running a fixed effects regression, the optimal share is about 11 %. The system GMM models treating the Share variables as exogenous or predetermined, on the other hand, would suggest an optimal share of between 13 and 15 %. Although focusing on competitiveness, taking cost effects into account, our results are in general in line with the findings of Beckmann and Kuhn (2009) and Hirsch and Mueller (2012).

4.5.3 Robustness Checks

Given the estimates results presented above, this subsection contains various robustness tests. As a first robustness check, we estimate the models outlined above outlined without controlling for the potential selection problem. Additionally, we estimate each model while reducing the sample to those firms that actually used temporary agency work at least once in the observation period. The results reported in Table 4.5 essentially confirm our previous findings. Regardless of the method applied or the sample used, we find a negative and significant coefficient for the variable Share and a significant positive coefficient for the Share2 variable, except for the system GMM models where Share and Share2 are treated as endogenous.

[19]Hansen tests for different subsets of instruments show that the rejection of the null hypothesis stems from a correlation between the error terms and the industry dummies. A correlation between the error terms and the industry dummies indicate, that the error terms vary systematically between the different industries.

Table 4.5 Estimation results using static and dynamic panel data models without controlling for the selection effect and a subsample of firms that used temporary agency work at least once

	Fixed effect	Sys GMM (1)	Sys GMM (2)	Sys GMM (3)	Fixed effect	Sys GMM (1)	Sys GMM (2)	Sys GMM (3)
Endogenous variable	ULC	ULC	ULC	ULC	ULC	ULC	ULC	ULC
Lag one of ULC		0.498***	0.495***	0.500***		0.493***	0.488***	0.498***
		(0.0187)	(0.0187)	(0.0188)		(0.0234)	(0.0233)	(0.0234)
Share	−0.121***	−0.0838***	−0.122***	−0.0481	−0.103***	−0.0642***	−0.106***	−0.0195
	(0.0138)	(0.0124)	(0.0225)	(0.0479)	(0.0136)	(0.0126)	(0.0231)	(0.0498)
Share2	1.110***	0.611***	0.990***	−0.0545	1.031***	0.536***	0.966***	−0.138
	(0.106)	(0.114)	(0.205)	(0.412)	(0.102)	(0.109)	(0.202)	(0.406)
Control variables	Yes	Yes	Yes	Yes	Yes	Yes	Yes	Yes
Year dummies	Yes	Yes	Yes	Yes	Yes	Yes	Yes	Yes
Industry dummies	Yes	Yes	Yes	Yes	Yes	Yes	Yes	Yes
Constant	−0.506***	0.106***	0.106***	0.107***	−0.518***	0.0144	0.0144	0.0166
	(0.0276)	(0.0127)	(0.0128)	(0.0127)	(0.0356)	(0.0150)	(0.0152)	(0.0150)
R-squared	0.179				0.210			
Number of ID	26,725	23,514	23,514	23,514	15,922	14,431	14,431	14,431
Observations	101,433	73,173	73,173	73,173	64,833	47,938	47,938	47,938
No. of instruments		46	60	58		46	60	58
Wald chi2		60920.52	59511.03	60281.66		45950.62	44476.86	45815.55
AR(2) test p-vlaues		0.302	0.299	0.323		0.311	0.309	0.332
Hansen test p-value		0.001	0.001	0.001		0.001	0.001	0.001
Optimal share	11.52 %	14.70 %	13.11 %	–	10.51 %	12.72 %	11.60 %	–

Robust standard errors in parentheses; Sys. GMM: Share variables treated as (1) exogenous, (2) predetermined, (3) endogenous
* p<0.1; ** p<0.05; *** p<0.01; Column (1)–(3): without selection control, Column (4)–(6): sub-sample of firms using temporary agency work at least once

Here again the coefficients of both Share variables are negative, but not significant. With respect to the quality of the GMM estimations, we have to note that the null hypothesis of the Hansen test is again rejected in all system GMM models of Table 4.5.

To take into account differences in the relationship between the use of temporary agency work and unit labor costs between different industries, we run separate models for eleven industry groups.[20] This may also help solve the problem of the results for the Hansen test in our results reported above, because the rejection of the null of the Hansen test could be a result of different misspecifications like heterogeneities in the sample. For each group two system GMM models are estimated. First we estimate a model including both Share variables and treat them as exogenous; second the estimations are done while treating the Share variables as endogenous. The respective results are provided in Table 4.6.

Due to space limitations, we only report the coefficients for the Share variables, their standard errors and general information for each estimation equation like the number of observations and several test statistics. For all models reported in Table 4.6, all control variables are included. The results of the industry group estimations are mixed. In five out of eleven groups (industries 20, 26, 29, 30t33 and 36), covering more than 40 % of all observations, the U-shaped relationship between share of temporary agency workers and unit labor costs is found, when the Share variables are treated as exogenous as well as endogenous. Both coefficients have the expected sign and are significant when treating them as exogenous. Treating them as endogenous, the coefficients still have the right signs, but most are insignificant. The reasons for the insignificance are increased standard errors when treating the Share variables as endogenous. But however, the point estimates in the model treating the Share variables as endogenous confirm the results of the model treating them as exogenous. Hence, for these five industry groups, the expected U-shaped relationship is found, even when the potential endogeneity of the Share variables is taken into account. For industry group 17t19 the expected U-shaped relationship between temporary agency work and unit labor costs is only found when both Share variables are treated as exogenous, while for the remaining groups no support for our hypothesis is found. The test for autocorrelation in error terms performs well in all models and the null hypothesis of the Hansen test cannot be rejected in most of the models. This robustness checks show that for some industry groups the expected U-shaped relationship between the use of temporary agency work und ULC is found even when the Hansen test perform well and potential endogeneity of the Share variables is taken into account.

Hence, most of our estimation results confirm the hypothesis of an (inverse) U-shaped relationship between the intensity of using temporary agency workers

[20]The classification of 11 groups is based on NACE rev. 1.1, as used, for example, by OECD STAN. To reduce the number of reported estimations within the respective table and to make sure that each industry group includes enough observations, we make use of this less detailed industry classification, compared to the one reported in Table 4.2.

Table 4.6 Estimation results for system GMM models for industry subgroups

Group	Share treatment	Coeff. Share	Std. Error	Coeff. Share2	Std. Error	N	Wald Chi	No. of Intstr.	Hansen p-value	AR(2) test p-value
15t16	Exogenous	−0.0581**	(0.0283)	0.178	(0.206)	8,819	14385.51	27	0.048	0.279
		−0.0324**	(0.0145)				14086.17	26	0.048	0.277
	Endogenous	−0.0426	(0.0621)	0.117	(0.319)		13919.24	39	0.068	0.278
		−0.0334	(0.0275)				13548.38	32	0.151	0.277
17t19	Exogenous	−0.163***	(0.0382)	0.967***	(0.168)	4,101	10315.43	28	0.293	0.611
		−0.00395	(0.0438)				10160.02	27	0.308	0.658
	Endogenous	0.198	(0.244)	−3.805	−2.823		10231.94	40	0.749	0.657
		−0.223	(0.156)				10265.23	33	0.441	0.573
20	Exogenous	−0.249***	(0.0756)	2.530***	(0.765)	1,938	3648.63	26	0.504	0.943
		−0.0720**	(0.0350)				3533.78	25	0.507	0.973
	Endogenous	−0.253	(0.225)	2.863	−2.297		3537.07	38	0.271	0.949
		−0.0543	(0.246)				3563.57	31	0.722	0.974
21t22	Exogenous	0.0856*	(0.0475)	−0.103	(0.342)	6,479	7094.02	27	0.435	0.818
		0.0728**	(0.0327)				7107.66	26	0.434	0.785
	Endogenous	0.373	(0.314)	−1.892	−2.593		6691.41	39	0.265	0.737
		0.209*	(0.124)				6957.65	32	0.727	0.64
23t25	Exogenous	−0.00930	(0.0264)	0.219	(0.268)	8,954	9746.03	28	0.085	0.18
		0.00994	(0.0156)				9763.36	27	0.088	0.177
	Endogenous	0.124	(0.112)	−0.0559	−1.222		9286.46	40	0.515	0.155
		0.101	(0.0625)				9475.97	33	0.521	0.158
26	Exogenous	−0.117***	(0.0435)	0.776***	(0.203)	3,770	1761.94	26	0.334	0.428
		−0.0152	(0.0327)				1774.05	25	0.36	0.42
	Endogenous	−0.136	(0.164)	1.488	−1.118		1748.00	38	0.521	0.447
		0.0593	(0.113)				1755.70	31	0.674	0.424

27t28	Exogenous	−0.0402	(0.0258)	0.675***	(0.202)	11,477	9321.16	27	0.544	0.835
		0.0422***	(0.0133)				9301.9	26	0.56	0.791
	Endogenous	0.203	(0.157)	−1.668	−1.285		9144.88	39	0.101	0.698
		0.0157	(0.0699)				9216.15	32	0.185	0.796
29	Exogenous	−0.175***	(0.0272)	1.051***	(0.205)	11,349	4918.14	26	0.027	0.377
		−0.0587***	(0.0150)				4762.85	25	0.034	0.391
	Endogenous	−0.139*	(0.0771)	0.819	(0.505)		4744.62	38	0.055	0.387
		−0.0643	(0.0502)				4725.18	31	0.028	0.388
30t33	Exogenous	−0.0936***	(0.0290)	0.653***	(0.226)	8,804	7489.89	29	0.001	0.986
		−0.0265	(0.0168)				7184.1	28	0.001	0.987
	Endogenous	−0.119	(0.130)	0.815	−1.233		7184.22	41	0.001	0.978
		−0.0196	(0.0830)				7149.19	34	0.001	0.987
34t35	Exogenous	−0.0601	(0.0386)	0.329	(0.264)	3,944	2124.35	27	0.075	0.993
		−0.0198	(0.0198)				2095.06	26	0.07	0.978
	Endogenous	−0.225	(0.152)	−0.103	−1.198		2108.12	39	0.075	0.86
		−0.238***	(0.0851)				2018.76	32	0.161	0.849
36	Exogenous	−0.243***	(0.0582)	2.166***	(0.519)	3,538	1478.59	26	0.246	0.668
		0.00735	(0.0476)				1533.07	25	0.23	0.473
	Endogenous	−0.249	(0.331)	0.998	−1.500		1498.58	38	0.124	0.45
		−0.113	(0.137)				1475.54	31	0.096	0.41

Robust standard errors in parentheses
* p<0.1; ** p<0.05; *** p<0.01; Industry Groups based on NACE rev. 2

and firm's ULC (competitiveness). This result is robust regardless of whether we account for the selection effect and treating the Share variables as exogenous or predetermined. Only for some industries the U-shaped relationship is found even when both Share variables are treated as endogenous. In general, most of our findings are in line with the results reported by Beckmann and Kuhn (2009) and Hirsch and Mueller (2012).

4.6 Conclusion

In this study the relationship between firm's competitiveness, measured as unit labor costs (ULC), and the intensity of using temporary agency workers is investigated. From the literature, we identify three main effects of the utilization temporary agency work on the competitiveness of companies. First, it is the increased flexibility in adjusting labor input to changes in demand that comes as a result of using temporary agency workers. This effect is always positive, no matter how high the share of temporary work on the input factor labor is. The second effect is the screening and motivation. Here, we find arguments that if temporary agency work is used to screen for new permanent employees it has a positive effect on the motivation and work performance of both temporary agency workers and permanent employees. This, however, changes if the share is too high and firms follow a strategy of substituting permanent staff with temporary agency workers. Finally, the temporary agency workers lack firm specific human capital. In this regard, temporary work has always a negative impact on the competitiveness of firms. Because of these opposing effects, we expect to find an (inverse) U-shaped relationship between the share of temporary agency work on total labor force and unit labor costs (competitiveness).

We test our hypothesis of a nonlinear dependency by regressing ULC on a proxy for the share of temporary agency work on total employment and the quadratic share as well as several controls. We control for firm specific effects by applying fixed effects regression models. To control for a potential selection into the use of this form of employment we apply a selection equation and the inverse Mills ratio. Moreover, we soften the assumption of strict exogeneity of independent variables by treating them as predetermined and endogenous while taking into account dynamic effects by using System GMM models.

We find an inverse U-shaped relationship between the intensity of temporary agency work used and the competitiveness of firms. The results are nearly stable regardless of the applied specification or estimation method. It follows that an increase in the share of temporary agency worker decreases ULC and, therefore, increases firms' competitiveness. This relationship, however, is not linear. The rising competitiveness turns into a declining one if the share of temporary agency worker increases too much. This nonlinear relationship allows us to calculate the optimal share of temporary agency work for different models. In the fixed effects model including the inverse Mills ratio to control for the selection bias, the estimated optimal share is about 11 %. Using dynamic panel date models gives an optimal share of about 13–15 % for the whole sample. The result of a U-shaped relationship is confirmed by various robustness checks.

However, the optimal shares should be interpreted carefully because the share of temporary agency workers in a firm is calculated using monetary information. Thus, the optimal share cannot be interpreted as a share in the number of employees. Nevertheless, our results show that firms can use temporary agency work to increase their competitiveness. Yet, the results also reveal that there is a rather low threshold and that a corporate strategy that aims to substitute permanent staff with temporary workers will not lead to greater competitiveness.

Chapter 5
Productivity in German Manufacturing Firms: Does Fixed-Term Employment Matter?

A growing proportion of employees are working under fixed-term contracts. This chapter empirically analyzes whether this strategy actually improves firm productivity. To this end, a large data set of German manufacturing firms and various panel data models are used in order to reveal the expected non-linear effect. The analysis also takes into account distortions that may result from selection into the use of fixed-term employment. The results of the investigation show that there is no significant effect of fixed-term employment on labor productivity when taking into account potential selection effects.

5.1 Introduction

The importance of fixed-term employment in Germany is constantly increasing. The share of fixed-term contracts for new hires increased from around 30 % in 2000 to about 45 % in 2010 (IAB 2011). Although approximately 50 % of all fixed-term contracts end with transfers into permanent contracts, the proportion of fixed-term workers in Germany is constantly increasing. In 2010 more than 9 % of all employees required to contribute to social security in Germany are employed under a fixed-term contract. In 2000 this figure was only about 6 % (Gundert and Hohendanner 2011). The increasing importance of this type of employment raises the question of whether and how it affects firm performance.

Previous research on temporary work and fixed-term contracts identifies two principle reasons for using this instrument. Firstly, the instrument is used to increase the external flexibility of labor input. Hence, severance payments and the like are not necessary, since expiring contracts simply reduce the number of employees

This chapter was originally co-authored with Alexander Schiersch.

S. Nielen, *Trade Credit and Temporary Employment*, Contributions to Management Science, DOI 10.1007/978-3-319-29850-4_5

through attrition when demand declines. Second, fixed-term contracts can be used to screen for productive workers. Thus, by selecting the latter and offering them permanent contracts, the overall quality and productivity of the workforce should increase.

However, within the labor market and management literature, the disadvantages of temporary work are also revealed. Here, it is mainly the demotivating effect that temporary work can have on both, temporary and permanent workers, when this instrument is abused. Moreover, the firm specific human capital of temporary workers is lower than that of permanent workers and firms have little incentive to invest in the training of temporary workers.

Since there are opposing effects of temporary work, its overall effect on firm performance is unclear. Previous literature on this topic is rare. Using sector aggregates, Damiani and Pompei (2010) analyzes the effect of labor protection on Total Factor Productivity (TFP) growth in 18 European countries between 1995 and 2005. They also control for the effect of growth in temporary employment on TFP, finding a negative and significant relation. Also using sectoral data, Auer et al. (2005) analyze the effect of employment tenure on productivity in 13 European countries for the 1992–2002 period. Their results show that productivity increases with increasing job tenure, but decreases after 13 years of job tenure. However, it follows for the case of fixed-term employees, that firms with a lower share of fixed-term worker should have a higher productivity. Making use of Spanish sectoral data from 1987 to 2000 Ortega and Marchante (2010) report a negative effect of temporary contracts only in the manufacturing and energy sector. For the remaining sectors no effects are found.

At the micro level, Cappellari et al. (2012) use 13,000 firm level observations of all Italian sectors between 2004 and 2007 in order to analyze the effects of deregulation reforms of apprenticeship and fixed-term contract. They find a small negative, but only weakly significant, effect of the reforms of fixed-term employment on labor productivity and must, therefore, reject their hypothesis that reforms in the legislation of fixed-term increase labor productivity. However, this result is in line with the findings of the two previously mentioned studies. Finally, Kleinknecht et al. (2006) analyze the effect of fixed-term employment using 590 Dutch firm observations. They find no significant effect of the percentage of personnel on fixed-term contracts on sales growth. In order to check the robustness of this finding, they also split the dataset into firms with active R&D and firms without active R&D. Again, in both subgroups no effect of the use of fixed-term employment on sales growth was found. Hence, previous empirical results point toward a weakly negative relationship with the exception of Kleinknecht et al. (2006).

This paper contributes to the literature by analyzing the effect of fixed-term employment on labor productivity for German manufacturing firms. In contrast to the aforementioned studies, we control for the inherent selection problem into using fixed-term contracts by means of the inverse Mills ratio, since some firms systematically do not use this instrument. Additionally, we apply dynamic panel data models to soften the assumption of strict exogeneity of explanatory variables.

The remainder of the paper is organized as follows. The subsequent section discusses related literature and derives the hypothesis. The data are introduced and first descriptive statistics are discussed in Sect. 5.2. The methods used in this study as well as the empirical strategy are introduced in Sect. 5.3 along with the empirical analysis. Section 5.4 provides a concluding discussion.

5.2 Theoretical Framework

In this section we present theoretical and empirical arguments to explain the relationship between the use of temporary employment and labor productivity. Within the extensive labor market and management literature, we identify three main factors and how they affect labor productivity. The first one is temporary employment as a tool to adjust the employment to product demand fluctuations. The second one is the screening aspect of temporary employment and the last one argues via firm specific human capital. At the end of this section we discuss how the different aspects might jointly affect labor productivity and derive the hypothesis.

5.2.1 Temporary Employment and Demand Fluctuations

In the case of demand fluctuation or a drop in demand, firms adjust all inputs accordingly. Yet, strict employment protection legislation (EPL) can "increase the cost of firing workers, thereby reducing the productivity threshold at which firms are willing to lay off worker" (Bassanini et al. 2009, p. 358). Hence, one reason why firms use temporary employment is because doing so allows for adjusting labor input when demand fluctuates while avoiding termination costs. One theory in this respect was developed by Nunziata and Staffolani (2007). It suggests that an increase in the demand for more flexible forms of employment is driven by increasing redundancy costs and volatile product demands. This is in line with the model of Bentolila and Saint-Paul (1992), which suggests that the demand for temporary employment is driven by fluctuations in product demand.

These theoretical considerations are confirmed by the survey of Houseman (2001) on reasons for using temporary employment. In it, the adjustment on demand fluctuations is named as the most important reason for using temporary employment. In the empirical part of the study, Houseman (2001) find a significant relationship between industry seasonality and the probability for using temporary work. Empirical evidence for the adjustment argument is also found by Vidal and Tigges (2009). Moreover, using data of establishments in Germany, Hagen (2003) reports that using fixed-term contracts increases the adjustment speed of work force to changes in product demand. Because the greater flexibility offered by fixed-term contracts helps to address changes in product demand, temporary work should have a positive effect on labor productivity. However, the effect of this instrument is limited because the termination of fixed-term workers without paying redundancy costs is only possible when the contract ends.

5.2.2 Temporary Employment and Screening

Another important aspect of fixed-term contracts is the fact that it can be used to screen for new productive workers or to substitute for core workers. According to principal agent theory, firms cannot observe the productivity of potential new employees before hiring them. Wang and Weiss (1998) provide a theoretical model in which firms use fixed-term contracts to screen new employees for a certain period. After the screening period the more productive employees will get open-ended contracts. This is congruent to the argument put forward by Lagos (2006). He argues that "economies with relatively high unemployment benefits will tend to exhibit relatively high levels of TFP" (Lagos 2006, 992). The reason is that if workers reservation wages increase, labor markets become tighter, "which in turn increases worker's outside option and raises measured TFP" (Lagos 2006, 992). The Total Factor Productivity (TFP) is rising because firms are no longer willing to accept low productivity and therefore are willing to hire only best matches and highly productive employees. One tool to find most productive workers is to use temporary employment for screening.

Using fixed-term contracts to screen potential new employees increases productivity in two ways. First, during the probation period the employee has an incentive to increase his/her effort in order to be offered an open-ended contract. This is confirmed by the findings of Engellandt and Riphahn (2005). They find that employees with a fixed-term contract have a higher probability to work unpaid overtime compared to employees with open-ended contracts. Moreover, Ichino and Riphahn (2005) show that job security after a probation period increases incentives for absenteeism. In turn, an increased probation period via temporary contracts might also serve as an incentive to be more productive. This is in line with the theoretical findings of Dolado and Stucchi (2008). Within their model they show that workers effort increases when the probability of getting a permanent contract increases. This positively affects TFP. However, they also point to other aspects of a high share of temporary workers that are not covered by the model but might have a negative effect on productivity (Dolado and Stucchi 2008). Second, offering open-ended contracts to only the most productive fixed-term contract employees will increase the productivity in the long run.

Empirical evidence for the screening argument is found by Gerfin et al. (2005) and Addison and Surfield (2009). Additionally results of Picchio (2008) show that a fixed-term contract can help employees obtain an open ended contract later on. For Germany, empirical evidence for the screening argument is reported by Boockmann and Hagen (2008). Gash (2008) find empirical evidence for fixed-term contracts to be a bridge to an open-ended contract. Moreover, McGinnity et al. (2005) show that fixed-term contracts are often used as a tool to screen new employees during the transition from education to work in West Germany. Using data from the German Socio-Economic Panel, Mertens and McGinnity (2004) find, that about 40 % of employees with a fixed-term contract have an open-ended contract 1 year later. Overall, empirical evidence for the use of temporary work as a sorting mechanism is given for Germany. However, in the case of Spain, where the labor market is highly segmented between temporary and permanent work, there is no evidence for the screening aspect of fixed-term employment (Amuedo-Dorantes 2000). Thus, the effect also depends on the structure and permeability of the labor market.

As mentioned above, fixed-term employees can also be used to substitute core workforce. Yet, this strategy comes with negative effects since it could lead to decreased motivation of both, fixed-term and existing core employees (Vidal and Tigges 2009). Decreasing motivation of employees with fixed-term contracts may result from lower job stability (Bergmann and Mertens 2011), lower job satisfaction (Bryson 2013) and lower wages (Mertens et al. 2007) compared to employees with permanent contracts. Lower motivation of core workers could be driven by decreasing trust in the commitment of the firm (George 2003). Less motivation of both types of workers could then result in lower labor productivity (Brown and Sessions 2005). This effect directly depends on the share of temporary workers on total work force of a firm. If the share of employees with fixed-term contracts is relatively high, employees fear a replacement strategy instead of screening and motivation may decrease (DeCuyper et al. 2008). Hence, with respect to screening and motivation, the effect of fixed-term workers on productivity depends on their share in total work force. On the one hand, a moderate use of fixed-term contracts should increase labor productivity due to the screening possibility and its positive motivational aspects. On the other hand, excessive use could negatively affect labor productivity because motivation of both types of workers decreases.

5.2.3 Temporary Employment and Human Capital

A third aspect of fixed-term contracts is the positive link between productivity and firm specific human capital. Theory suggests that investments in firm specific human capital depend on labor market conditions. In an extension of his model on labor markets with search friction and firing costs, Wasmer (2006) analysis the incentives of firms to invest in human capital. Referring to Becker (1964), he implies that firms are willing to partly or fully subsidies training costs. In a perfectly free labor market firms do not gain. Yet, in a labor market with low turnover rates due strong EPL (e.g. high firing costs), as for instance the German labor market, "firms gain from fostering specific skills acquisition by gaining more productivity" (Wasmer 2006, 821). However, investing in firm specific human capital becomes profitable in the long run. Hence, if the contract of employees ends after a relative short period, there is little incentive for firms to invest in the firm specific human capital of these employees. Therefore an increasing share of fixed-term contracts on total work force should go in line with decreasing investments in firm specific human capital.

Empirical evidence for a negative relationship between temporary work and investing in human capital is reported by Arulampalam et al. (2004). Also Booth et al. (2002b) find that employees with temporary jobs receive less training than employees with open-ended contracts. Moreover, findings of Shire et al. (2009) suggest that firms offering further training tend to make use of long term contracts instead of temporary employment. The same is reported by Albert et al. (2005). They find that firms that do not provide vocational training have higher shares of temporary worker compared to firms offering further training. Their results also show that given that a firm provides on the job training, employees with temporary contracts have a lower probability of receiving training compared to the ones with open-ended contracts. Yet, as shown by Zwick (2006) for the German case, on-the-job training enhances firm productivity. Moreover, employees receiving training are also more satisfied with their job and, therefore, have a higher job performance (Jones et al. 2009). Regarding the relationship of fixed-term employment and the incentive to invest in human capital, an increasing share of employees with temporary contracts reduces labor productivity due to lower investments in firm specific human capital.

5.2.4 Temporary Employment and Labor Productivity

Summing up, we find arguments for a positive as well as for a negative relationship between the share of fixed-term workers in an establishment and its productivity. First, regarding flexibility, using temporary employment should increase labor productivity via increasing flexibility in case of product demand changes. However, positive effects resulting from an increased flexibility are restricted because employees with a fixed-term contract can only be laid off without paying redundancy costs when the contract expires. Second, a moderate use of fixed-term employment to screen for productive employees should increase labor productivity. An extensive use in order to replace core workers with temporary ones may reduce labor productivity due to the decreased motivation of both types of employees. Third, an increasing share of fixed-term employees should be accompanied with decreasing labor productivity because the incentive to invest in firm specific human capital is lower compared to permanent employees as human capital and productivity are positively linked. Combining these arguments, the overall effect of the share of fixed-term employees on labor productivity depends on the share of fixed-term contracts on total work force of an establishment. Table 5.1 compares the expected effects of fixed-term employment on labor productivity for low and high shares.

The expected effect of fixed-term employment on labor productivity depends on the intensity temporary employment is used: a moderate use of fixed-term contracts should increase labor productivity due to increasing flexibility of labor input and the possibility to screen for productive employees, both overcoming the negative effect

Table 5.1 Channels and expected overall effect

Channel	Low share	High share
Flexibility	+	+
Screening	+	−
Human capital	−	−
Overall effect	+	−

of lower firm specific human capital; an intensive use should have a negative effect on labor productivity because both types of employees are less motivated and fixed-term contract employees tend to have lower human capital, both overcompensating the positive effect of a higher flexibility of labor input. With an increasing share of fixed-term employees in total workforce, the positive effects on productivity became less effective and negative effects became more effective. At some point positive and negative effects cancel each other out. When increasing the share of fixed-term employees above this threshold, the negative effects exceed positive effects. Hence, our hypothesis is that the relationship between the intensity of using fixed-term workers and labor productivity is inverse U-shaped.[1]

5.3 Data

5.3.1 Sample

The study uses IAB Establishment Panel data for the 2004–2009 period. The data are gathered and compiled by the German Federal Employment Agency (*Bundesagentur für Arbeit*). It is an annual survey covering about 15,500 establishments per year, designed to be representative both for average and for longitudinal analysis (Fischer et al. 2009). The questionnaire includes questions about staff development, personnel requirements, sales, investment, exports, as well as R&D, innovation and organizational change (Bellmann et al. 2002). In addition, there are specific questions addressing the different forms of employment used by the firm, such as temporary agency work or fixed-term employment. Altogether, the dataset contains about 320 variables, which, however, are mostly related to labor market issues.[2]

[1]The hypothesis of an inverse U-shaped relationship between temporary employment and firm performance is in line with the one formulated by Nielen and Schiersch (2014) and Hirsch and Mueller (2012) for the case of temporary agency work.

[2]The questionnaire can be downloaded for each year. See http://fdz.iab.de/en/FDZ_Establishment_Data/IAB_Establishment_Panel/IAB_Establishment_Panel_Working_Tools.aspx. Moreover, Städele and Müller (2006) provide a detailed description for each variable up to 2005.

In order to create a panel, the IAB provides a STATA and SPSS syntax that has to be applied on the data to combine the waves.[3] In these programs some variables are treated to ensure comparability over time since the questionnaire has changed slightly over time. We refrain from discussing every code line here as the interested reader can find each individual step in the syntax and the detailed description of every variable for each year in Städele and Müller (2006). After the recoding and renaming has taken place, the waves are merged into a single dataset creating a panel. In this step, the procedure of the IAB also includes the transformation of values between 2 years. This takes place for organizational variables that refer to changes in past years.[4]

However, one significant challenge, unresolved by the IAB procedure, remains. Within each survey, questions focus on different time horizons. More specifically, the questions on turnover, foreign sales, sources of founding, sum of investments etc. refer to the previous year. The questions on the business development in the next year, plans to change the number of employees, plans to produce abroad , to invest in EU countries etc. refer to the next year. Moreover, a number of the questions, mainly on inputs, for example on the number of employees liable to social security, the number of skilled workers, the number of unskilled workers, the number of temporary employees and of fixed term employees etc. refer to June 30th of the year that the survey took place.[5] Hence, even after the IAB procedure, data for an establishment in specific year refer to different years. This means, for example, that the data assigned to year/wave 2001 contain the turnover for the year 2000, the number of employees refers to the year 2001 and the investment plans refer to 2002. Hence, during data preparation, we must ensure that data are correctly assigned to the year that they reflect.

In order to resolve the time dimension problem, we adapt the IAB procedure and transfer establishment data of wave $t+1$, which refer to the situation in t, to the very same establishments in wave t. This is possible because each establishment has a unique ID, which ensures that the data for each establishment in a year belongs to that very year. However, this also means that we lose 2009 from the analysis, since some of the data collected in 2009 belongs to 2008; for example

[3]http://fdz.iab.de/en/FDZ_Establishment_Data/IAB_Establishment_Panel/IAB_Establishment_Panel_Working_Tools.aspx

[4]This is done for the variables *responsibilities, team work, reliance on internal labour, Expansion of purchase of products, Restructuring of procurement, Restructuring of departments, Ecological measures in enterprise, Improvement of quality management, etc*. For more details and every variable see the syntax in the STATA file 5̌_Transfer_of_values.doävailable at http://fdz.iab.de/en/FDZ_Establishment_Data/IAB_Establishment_Panel/IAB_Establish-ment_Panel_Working_Tools.aspx

[5]The questionnaires for each year can be downloaded at http://fdz.iab.de/en/FDZ_Establishment_Data/IAB_Establishment_Panel/IAB_Establishment_Panel_Working_Tools.aspx

turnover, which is transferred to 2008.[6] Thus, the dataset covers the period 2004–2008. Furthermore, we only include firms with at least five employees. The reason for this is the German Employment Protection Act, a law that applies only to firms with fewer than 5 employees. Below that threshold, firms can rather easily hire and fire people. Hence, in these firms there is no need for fixed-term employment to increase flexibility or even screen newly hired workers.[7] Including firms with less than 5 employees will, therefore, bias the analysis. Since this study focuses on manufacturing establishments, all non-manufacturing establishments are excluded. Finally, all firms with fewer than three observations are excluded in the latter analysis in order to apply panel data models. The final sample consists of 8787 observations from 2244 manufacturing establishments.

5.3.2 *Measurement of Variables*

The dependent variable in the analysis is the log of labor productivity (*LaborProd*), which is calculated as real sales per capita. The deflation is done using sectoral producer price indices of the OECD for Germany. The regressor of interest is the log of the share of fixed-term employed on total employees (*Share*). Here, neither the number of temporary agency workers nor interns are taken into account. The reason is that both numbers are asked for as date data. We know, however, that the job duration of 50 % of all temporary agency workers in client firms is less than 3 month. Interns in Germany work between 1 and 6 months. Hence, although we might find temporary agency workers or interns on the 30th of June, it is highly possible that they have not been in the firms in the beginning of a year and that they will not be there through the end of a year. Simply adding them to the number of employees would therefore cause the analysis to be biased.[8] For the so-constructed variable, we expect the coefficients of *Share* to be significantly positive if the theoretical remarks of Sect. 5.1 hold true. Moreover, since the effect might be non-linear, the variable is also included in the analysis with its squared values (*Share2*) and the respective coefficient is expected to be negative.

In addition to these regressors, we include the logarithms of the following control variables: the overall number of employees to capture the size of the firms (*Size*); the proportion of intermediate inputs on sales (*Intermediate*) to capture the position

---

[6]However, even if we would forgo this step and work with lagged independent variables, 2009 would be lost since we would need the data of wave 2010, since the output of 2009 is captured in the wave 2010.

[7]As part of the 2004 Hartz IV reforms, the threshold increased to 10 employees. However, the transitional rules imply that for companies with more than 5 "old" workers, the former limit of 5 employees still applies. Hence, we kept the limit of 5 employees.

[8]We estimate models including the share of temporary agency workers as control variable. Our results are not affected by this robustness check. The respective results are available upon request from the authors.

of the firms in the value chain; the share of qualified employees on total labor force (*Qualified*) to catch the human capital intensity of production; the share of part time worker in the company (*Part time*) as an additional control variable for the employment structure; the share of exports on sales (*Export*) to take into account the range of business activities of firms; and finally the investments per capita (*Investment*), which captures investments in ICT capital, production equipment, buildings and the like, as proxy for the capital intensity of production.

Additional control variables in the analysis are the following dummy variables: the age of the companies (*Age1-Age5*) for companies younger than 5 years, 5–9 years, 10–14 years, 15–19 years, and 20 or more years; a dummy variable that equals one if a company closed a part of the firm within the last year (*Closed*); a dummy variable if a part of the firm was outsourced (*Outsourced*); if a spin-off has taken place (*Spin*); a dummy variable that becomes one if a part of another company was integrated (*Integrated*); dummy variables if the majority owner is East German (*Owned1*), West German (*Owned2*), a foreigner (*Owned3*), is the state (*Owned4*), has no majority owner (*Owned5*) or if the majority owner is unknown (*Owned6*); dummy variables for each of the 16 industries in the analysis; as well as sixteen dummy variables for federal states the establishments are located in; dummy variables for companies with sectoral collective agreement, company collective agreement and no collective agreement (*Tarif1-Tarif3*); and a dummy variable taking the value of one if a company has a work council (*WorkConcil*).

Table 5.2 provides descriptive statistics for all continuous explanatory variables and for the dependent variable labor productivity, distinguishing between within and between variation and Table 5.3 contains simple descriptive statistics for the dummy variables. For most variables between variation exceeds within variation. Interestingly for *Share* the between variation is only a little higher. Hence, the share of fixed-term employees changes considerably over time and not just between establishments.

Table 5.4 reveals the regional distribution of observations and Table 5.5 contains the descriptive statistics of the share of fixed-term employment per industry. From Table 5.4 it can be seen that 4377 establishments are located in West Germany, while 4126 are located in East Germany and Berlin is the location of 284 establishments. The mean share is rather low, ranging from 2 to 5 % in the entire data set. But among those firms that used fixed-term employment, the mean ranges from 5.2 to 13 %. Moreover, the maximum share ranges from 26 to almost 100 %. Thus, fixed-term employment is a significant input factor and is occasionally heavily used. Finally, since some firms have never used this instrument, the analysis is subject to a selection problem.

Table 5.2 Descriptive statistics: continuous variables

Variable		Mean	Std. Dev.	Min	Max	N	
LaborProd	Overall	150988.5	184445.4	76.90006	2724388	N =	8787
	Between		175498.6	7563.579	2220908	n =	2244
	Within		44082.6	−460682.5	1190880	T-bar =	3.91578
Share	Overall	0.0367837	0.0749916	0	0.9931973	N =	8787
	Between		0.0608276	0	0.6739306	n =	2244
	Within		0.0471705	−0.4767171	0.768491	T-bar =	3.91578
Size	Overall	231.2081	1261.51	5	46140	N =	8787
	Between		1460.919	5	45024.67	n =	2244
	Within		57.47266	−1493.792	2099.008	T-bar =	3.91578
Qualified	Overall	0.7055241	0.2322374	0	1	N =	8787
	Between		0.2117569	0	1	n =	2244
	Within		0.1018012	−0.0224171	1.399363	T-bar =	3.91578
Part time	Overall	0.0992271	0.1435632	0	1	N =	8787
	Between		0.1306716	0	0.9706714	n =	2244
	Within		0.0646558	−0.653587	0.7658938	T-bar =	3.91578
Export	Overall	0.1901104	0.257645	0	1	N =	8787
	Between		0.2495662	0	1	n =	2244
	Within		0.0686554	−0.3598896	0.9101104	T-bar =	3.91578
Investment	Overall	5903.908	14799.74	0	714285.7	N =	8787
	Between		12518.02	0	410714.3	n =	2244
	Within		10215.98	−297667.5	309475.3	T-bar =	3.91578

(continued)

Table 5.2 (continued)

Variable		Mean	Std. Dev.	Min	Max	N	
Intermediate	Overall	52.72061	19.09313	1	100	N =	8787
	Between		17.27151	3.8	100	n =	2244
	Within		9.056647	5.97061	106.0539	T-bar =	3.91578
Mills ratio	Overall	1.82969	0.278848	1.595769	4.494524	N =	8787
	Between		0.2861854	1.595813	4.48323	n =	2244
	Within		0.0513003	1.184234	2.240196	T-bar =	3.91578

Notes: No. of observations: 8787; No. of establishments: 2244

Table 5.3 Descriptive statistics: dummy variables

Variable	Mean	Std. Dev.	Min	Max	N
Age1	0.0458632	0.2092003	0	1	8787
Age2	0.0888813	0.2845885	0	1	8787
Age3	0.1903949	0.3926350	0	1	8787
Age4	0.1301923	0.3365341	0	1	8787
Age5	0.5446683	0.4980291	0	1	8787
Closed	0.0125185	0.1111899	0	1	8787
Outsourced	0.0133151	0.1146269	0	1	8787
Spin	0.0070559	0.0837072	0	1	8787
Integrated	0.0256060	0.1579658	0	1	8787
Owned1	0.2998748	0.4582290	0	1	8787
Owned2	0.5712985	0.4949186	0	1	8787
Owned3	0.0995789	0.2994548	0	1	8787
Owned4	/	/	/	/	/
Owned5	0.0179811	0.1328902	0	1	8787
Owned6	0.0091044	0.0949868	0	1	8787
West	0.50643	0.4999871	0	1	8787
Tarif1	0.3737339	0.4838218	0	1	8787
Tarif2	0.0938887	0.2916904	0	1	8787
Tarif3	0.5323774	0.498979	0	1	8787
WorkConcil	0.3996813	0.4898607	0	1	8787

Notes: Due to the private policy rules of the IAB, the descriptive statistics of some variables are not publishable due to the small number of cases in the respective subgroups

Table 5.4 Descriptive statistics: federal states

State	N	Percent
Schleswig-Holstein	183	2.08
Hamburg	60	0.68
Lower Saxony	766	8.72
Bremen	198	2.25
North Rhine-Westphalia	838	9.54
Hesse	468	5.33
Baden-Württemberg	782	8.90
Bavaria	600	6.83
Saarland	134	1.52
Rhineland-Palatinate	348	3.96
West	4377	49.86
Berlin	284	3.23
Brandenburg	593	6.75
Mecklenburg-Western Pomerania	389	4.43
Saxony	1210	13.77
Saxony-Anhalt	773	8.80
Thuringia	1161	13.21
East	4126	46.91
Total	8787	100

Table 5.5 Descriptive statistics: share per industry

	All firms					Only firms using fixed-term contracts				
Industry	Obs	Mean	Std. Dev.	Min	Max	Obs	Mean	Std. Dev.	Min	Max
Food/luxury	949	0.0450	0.0999	0.0000	0.9500	438	0.0976	0.1285	0.0034	0.9500
Textiles/clothing	273	0.0350	0.0674	0.0000	0.4348	127	0.0753	0.0821	0.0034	0.4348
Paper/printing/	451	0.0273	0.0671	0.0000	0.8451	198	0.0622	0.0901	0.0016	0.8451
Wood sector	477	0.0282	0.0777	0.0000	0.9756	141	0.0956	0.1185	0.0062	0.9756
Chemical/pharmaceutical sector	521	0.0415	0.0701	0.0000	0.6000	309	0.0699	0.0793	0.0022	0.6000
Plastics industry	483	0.0465	0.0733	0.0000	0.8667	312	0.0721	0.0805	0.0025	0.8667
Glass/stones/ore extraction	483	0.0450	0.0831	0.0000	0.6667	235	0.0924	0.0992	0.0011	0.6667
Manufacture of basic metals	645	0.0429	0.0861	0.0000	0.9932	358	0.0772	0.1034	0.0005	0.9932
Recycling	93	0.0381	0.0826	0.0000	0.4500	27	0.1313	0.1070	0.0152	0.4500
Manufacture of fabricated metal	1202	0.0320	0.0528	0.0000	0.4688	540	0.0711	0.0585	0.0020	0.4688
Machinery and equipment	1283	0.0281	0.0457	0.0000	0.4286	693	0.0520	0.0512	0.0009	0.4286
Motor vehicles, trailers and semitrailers	366	0.0484	0.0645	0.0000	0.3804	245	0.0724	0.0670	0.0013	0.3804
Other vehicle production	147	0.0493	0.1213	0.0000	0.8333	82	0.0884	0.1517	0.0021	0.8333
Manufacture of electrical equipment	590	0.0388	0.0711	0.0000	0.5238	303	0.0755	0.0841	0.0025	0.5238
Precision and optical equipment	522	0.0207	0.0391	0.0000	0.2642	194	0.0556	0.0467	0.0026	0.2642
Furniture, jewelry/toys	302	0.0497	0.1392	0.0000	0.9524	120	0.1251	0.1988	0.0029	0.9524

5.4 Empirical Investigation

The analysis of the relationship between the use of fixed-term contracts and labor productivity is presented in three steps. First is our estimation strategy. We follow with our main results, and then, some robustness checks are presented.

5.4.1 Methods and Empirical Strategy

To control for the potential self-selection into the use of fixed-term contracts, the empirical estimation starts with the estimation of a probit selection model. The dependent variable takes the value of one if a company uses fixed-term contracts and zero otherwise. Based on the result of the probit model we calculate the inverse Mills ratio. This ratio is used as an additional variable in the regression models to control for the selection effect. For detailed discussion of this approach see Briggs (2004). To increase identification of the model and to avoid potential multicollinearity between the inverse Mills ratio and the explanatory variables of the regression models we make use of exclusion restriction as proposed by Puhani (2000). This means, we exclude some variables used in the selection model from the regression models in the second stage.

For the exclusion restriction we use dummy variables for the varying types of collective agreement. The data distinguishes between three different types of collective agreement: industrial collective agreement, company agreement and no collective agreement. We argue that establishments have different probabilities of using fixed-term employment depending upon whether they have collective agreements or not. Establishments with industrial collective agreements are expected to be more likely to use temporary contracts, because fixed-term contracts can be used to avoid the strict employment regulations that result from collective agreements. In case of a company agreement, the use of fixed-term employment is often regulated by agreement. Hence, establishments with a company agreement are expected to be less likely to use fixed-term employment because the agreement restricts the use of this kind of employment. In the first stage the dummy variables for company agreement and no collective agreement are included in the selection equation to estimate the probability of using fixed-term employment. The dummy for industrial collective agreement is the respective reference category.[9]

[9]Additionally, we use two alternative exclusion restrictions and estimate one model without an exclusion restriction in order to check whether our results are affected by changes in the exclusion restriction. First, we use six different dummy variables for legal status and second, a combination of collective agreement and legal status dummies are used. Finally, we estimate the selection equation without an exclusion restriction. However, the results of our second stage regression models are not affected by changes in the exclusion restriction. The respective results are available upon request from the authors.

To test the hypothesis of an inverse U-shaped relationship between the use of fixed-term employment and labor productivity, the following equation is estimated:

$$log(LabProd_{it}) = \beta_1 Share_{it} + \beta_2 Share2_{it} + \gamma_k log(x_{kit}) + \theta_m D_{mit} + \delta Mills_{it} + v_i + u_{it}$$

with $i = 1, \ldots, N, t = 1, \ldots, T, Share = log(1+Share)$ and $Share2 = 0.5*Share^2$. $Share_{it}$ is the quotient of employees with a fixed-term contract and total work force of an establishment. X_{kit} denotes all continuous control variables, D_{mit} indicates all dummy variables including year dummies and $Mills_{it}$ captures the self-selection into the use of fixed-term employment via inverse Mills ratio. Finally with v_i denotes an establishment specific fixed effect and u_{it} is the error term capturing unsystematic influences of labor productivity.

The estimation strategy is as follows: To get a first impression of how the use of fixed-term contracts and labor productivity are related, we start with estimating a simple OLS regression model. In order to exploit the panel structure of the data and to control for correlation between unobserved fixed effects and the explanatory variables, we then apply a fixed effect regression model. Finally we estimate two specifications of a system GMM model to account for dynamic effects and possible endogeneity of explanatory variables resulting from a correlation with past error terms.

To overcome the potential weak instrument problem of the first difference GMM estimator proposed by Arellano and Bond (1991), we apply the system GMM estimator implemented by Arellano and Bover (1995) and by Blundell and Bond (1998). All system GMM models are estimated by using the package provided by Roodman (2009a). Following Roodman (2009b), we reduce the number of instruments by using the collapse option. In the first specification all explanatory variables are treated to be exogenous. In the second specification, both share variables are treated as predetermined. Thus, they are assumed to be potentially correlated with past error terms but not with current ones. The lagged dependent variable is endogenous by the nature of the model and is therefore instrumented with own lags starting with lag order two. For all system GMM specifications p-values of the Hansen test of over-identifying restrictions and p-values of a test for second order autocorrelation of the error terms in differences are reported. We are aware of the fact that applying panel data models does not necessary allow for a causal interpretation of the results. This is the case even if the strong assumption of strict endogeneity of explanatory variables is relaxed by using system GMM models.

For a first robustness check the fixed effects model and both system GMM specifications are estimated without controlling for the inherent selection into the use of fixed-term contracts. To take into account differences between West and East Germany, we apply separate estimations for both groups. This estimations again cover the fixed effects model and both system GMM specifications.

5.4.2 Estimation Results

The analysis starts by calculating the inverse Mills ratio to account for potential self-selection into the use of fixed-term contracts. The corresponding estimation results of the probit model are outlined in column one of Table 5.6. In accordance with Kleinknecht et al. (2006), we find a positive coefficient for firm size and a negative one for the share of qualified employees.

The actual analysis of the relationship between labor productivity and the share of fixed-term employees in total workforce starts with an OLS model in column two, followed by a fixed effects model in column three of Table 5.6. In both estimates, we find a positive but insignificant coefficient for the *Share* variable as well as a negative coefficient for the *Share2* variable. The coefficient for *Share2* is weakly significant only in the fixed effects model. Hence, the results rather indicate the existence of a weakly negative relationship between labor productivity and the use of fixed-term employment than the existence of an inverse U-shaped relationship. Column 4 and 5 contain the estimates of the system GMM approaches. In column 4, all regressors are modeled as exogenous, except the lagged dependent variable, while in the second system GMM model both *Share* and *Share2* variables are assumed to be predetermined. We treat both *Share* and *Share2* variables this way in order to check whether previous results are affected by potential endogeneity resulting from a correlation between the share variables and past error terms. In both estimates, however, we find negative, but insignificant coefficients for *Share* and *Share2*. This implies, first, that the imposed inverse U-shaped relationship is rejected by both estimations and, second, that the potentially negative but weak relationship, as found in the fixed effect model, finds only weak support. In general, the results of our basic models do not support the hypothesis of an inverse U-shaped relationship between the share of fixed-term employees on total work force and labor productivity.

Because the expected inverse U-shaped relationship between the use of fixed-term employment and labor productivity is not found and some results suggest a weak negative relationship between both, we estimate the same regression models without including the *Share2* variable. The respective results are shown in Table 5.7.

In all models the coefficient of *Share* is negative, but only significant in the system GMM model treating all the share variable as exogenous. Thus our results provide no evidence for an inverse U-shaped relationship, nor for a positive or negative relationship. Thus, it follows that the share of employees with fixed-term contracts on total work force of an establishment has no significant impact on labor productivity.

With respect to the remaining control variables, *Size* is found to have negative and positive parameters, depending on the applied empirical method. In contrast, we find that when *Intermediate* is larger there is a positive effect on labor productivity in all estimates. This, however, might only control for the effect that higher turnovers are generated by using more intermediate inputs, which translates into higher productivity here, since labor productivity is defined as sales per capita. Another variable with significant coefficients in all models is *Export*. Hence, firms with a

Table 5.6 Estimation results with controlling for the selection into fixed-term employment via inverse Mills ratio

Variable	1	2	3	4	5
L1 LaborProd				0.4179***	0.4236***
				(0.0782)	(0.0779)
Share		0.1033	0.2010	−0.0045	−0.0063
		(0.1958)	(0.1293)	(0.1480)	(0.2634)
Share2		−1.4321	−1.2969*	−0.9245	−1.3010
		(1.1576)	(0.7177)	(0.7394)	(1.2686)
Size	0.6263***	0.0603***	−0.3430***	0.0382***	0.0380***
	(0.0212)	(0.0072)	(0.0443)	(0.0107)	(0.0108)
Intermediate	0.1074***	0.4171***	0.0363***	0.2130***	0.2115***
	(0.0404)	(0.0171)	(0.0136)	(0.0274)	(0.0273)
Qualified	−0.3991***	0.5342***	0.0440	0.2969***	0.2943***
	(0.1224)	(0.0517)	(0.0382)	(0.0602)	(0.0603)
Part time	0.0533	−1.5038***	−0.1316	−0.7436***	−0.7373***
	(0.1677)	(0.0706)	(0.0582)	(0.1206)	(0.1204)
Export	0.3446***	0.4401***	0.2845***	0.3163***	0.3145***
	(0.1032)	(0.0433)	(0.0647)	(0.0613)	(0.0610)
Investment	0.0192***	0.0222***	0.0042***	0.0071***	0.0070***
	(0.0048)	(0.0020)	(0.0012)	(0.0019)	(0.0019)
Company agreement	−0.1580***				
	(0.0594)				
No agreement	−0.0570				
	(0.0397)				
Mills		0.0363	0.4000***	0.0269	0.0262
		(0.0223)	(0.0934)	(0.0272)	(0.0272)
Age dummies	Yes	Yes	Yes	Yes	Yes
Industry dummies	Yes	Yes	Yes	Yes	Yes
Restructuring dummies		Yes	Yes	Yes	Yes
Federal state dummies	Yes	Yes	Yes	Yes	Yes
Year dummies	Yes	Yes	Yes	Yes	Yes
Ownership dummies	Yes	Yes	Yes	Yes	Yes
Work council	Yes	Yes	Yes	Yes	Yes
Constant	−2.7274***	8.9692***	11.9967***	5.3211****	5.2701***
	(0.2347)	(0.1005)	(0.3339)	(0.7503)	(0.7469)
No. of observations	8787	8787	8787	6182	6182
No. ID			2244	2121	2121
(Pseudo) R−squared	0.3203	0.5102	0.1272		
Wald chi2	2503.92***			7625.51***	7764.43***
No. of instruments				61	69
Hansen test p−value				0.439	0.205
AR(2) test p−value				0.940	0.924

Notes: Robust standard errors in parentheses
* p<0.1; ** p<0.05; *** p<0.01
Columns: (1): Probit; (2): OLS; (3): FE; (4): SysGMM exogen; (5): SysGMM predetermined

Table 5.7 Estimation results with controlling for the selection into fixed-term employment via inverse Mills ratio

Variable	1	2	3	4
L1 LaborProd			0.4195***	0.4215***
			(0.0779)	(0.0779)
Share	−0.1301	−0.0108	−0.1543**	−0.2342
	(0.1171)	(0.0741)	(0.0779)	(0.1652)
Size	0.0612***	−0.3398***	0.0387***	0.0394***
	(0.0073)	(0.0442)	(0.0107)	(0.0110)
Intermediate	0.4173***	0.0370***	0.2126***	0.2122***
	(0.0171)	(0.0137)	(0.0274)	(0.0273)
Qualified	0.5339***	0.0448	0.2943***	0.2922***
	(0.0517)	(0.0381)	(0.0599)	(0.0601)
Part time	−1.5077***	−0.1336**	−0.7418***	−0.7390***
	(0.0707)	(0.0579)	(0.1202)	(0.1202)
Export	0.4405***	0.2834***	0.3160***	0.3161***
	(0.0433)	(0.0647)	(0.0612)	(0.0611)
Investment	0.0223***	0.0043***	0.0071***	0.0071***
	(0.0020)	(0.0012)	(0.0019)	(0.0019)
Mills	0.0354	0.4066***	0.0260	0.0248
	(0.0223)	(0.0936)	(0.0272)	(0.0273)
Age dummies	Yes	Yes	Yes	Yes
Industry dummies	Yes	Yes	Yes	Yes
Restructuring dummies	Yes	Yes	Yes	Yes
Federal state dummies	Yes	Yes	Yes	Yes
Year dummies	Yes	Yes	Yes	Yes
Ownership dummies	Yes	Yes	Yes	Yes
Work council	Yes	Yes	Yes	Yes
Constant	8.9674***	11.9632***	5.3049***	5.2889***
	(0.1004)	(0.3343)	(0.7474)	(0.7472)
No. of observations	8787	8787	6182	6182
No. ID		2244	2121	2121
R-squared	0.5101	0.1263		
Wald chi2			7650.26***	7694.62***
No. of instruments			60	64
Hansen test p-value			0.438	0.362
AR(2) test p-value			0.941	0.934

Notes: Robust standard errors in parentheses
* p<0.1; ** p<0.05; *** p<0.01
Columns: (1): OLS; (2): FE; (3): SysGMM exogen; (4): SysGMM predet

higher share on turnover abroad have a higher productivity. Moreover, an increasing share of *Qualified* does also increase the productivity. Only in the fixed effect model the respective coefficient is not significant. The coefficient of *Part time* is negative and significant in all models. The coefficient of *Investment* is positive and significant in all models. The signs and magnitude of the coefficients of all control variables are not or only barely affected whether *Share2* is included or not.

With respect to the selection effect, we find the expected. The coefficient of the inverse Mills ratio is significant in the fixed effect approach. Hence, the estimation results are subject to a selection effect. Moreover, the coefficients of the inverse Mills ratio in the System GMM approach are not significant. This is what we expect, since by including the lagged dependent variable in the regression, a part of the distortion resulting from the selection is already captured.

In all system GMM estimations shown in Tables 5.6 and 5.7, the null hypothesis of the Hansen test of over-identifying can not be rejected at a 5 % level. Also the p-value of the test for autocorrelation is above 5 %. This implies that, in general, the moment conditions are valid and the error terms are not auto correlated.

5.4.3 Robustness Checks

Table 5.8 contains three robustness checks. In the first part the results without controlling for possible selection into the use of fixed-term employment via inverse Mills ratio are shown. The second and third parts provide separate estimation results for subsamples using only establishments located in West and East Germany. For each robustness check the fixed effects model and both system GMM specifications are estimated with and without *Share2*, the squared term of the share variable. In all models only the coefficients of *Share* and *Share2* as well as the number of observations and diagnostic statistics are reported. Control variables included in our base line models reported in Tables 5.6 and 5.7 are also included in all models, but the respective coefficients are not reported here.[10]

Ignoring the problem of a potential selection effect leads to the expected inverse U-shaped relationship in the fixed effects model. The coefficient *Share* is positive while the coefficient of *Share2* is negative. Both are significant at the 5 % level. But, however, in both system GMM models both *Share* and *Share2* have negative, but not significant, coefficients. Therefore, the same models are estimated without including *Share2*. The respective coefficient of *Share* is negative in all three models, but only significant in the first system GMM model, which treats all explanatory variables as exogenous except the lagged dependent variable. It follows that ignoring the selection effect would lead to incorrect conclusions regarding the relationship between productivity and the share of fixed-term workers.

---

[10]The coefficients are available upon request from the authors.

Table 5.8 Robustness checks

	Share	Share2	N	R-squared/ Wald chi2	No. of Inst.	Hansen test p-value	AR(2) test p-value
Without controlling for potential selection into the use of fixed-term contracts							
FE	0.2730** (0.1279)	−1.5532** (0.7152)	8787	0.1173			
GMM_a	−0.0129 (0.1480)	−0.9048 (0.7395)	6182	7620.28***	60	0.434	0.934
GMM_b	−0.0089 (0.2631)	−1.2969 (1.2701)	6182	7758.73***	68	0.202	0.918
FE	0.0089 (0.0747)		8787	0.1161			
GMM_a	−0.1594** (0.0768)		6182	7644.70***	59	0.432	0.935
GMM_b	−0.2360 (0.1651)		6182	7689.13***	63	0.361	0.929
Only establishments located in West Germany (with selection control)							
FE	0.1457 (0.1411)	−0.5055 (0.5915)	4377	0.1795			
GMM_a	0.0455 (0.1821)	−1.8451** (0.8954)	3029	12008.36***	55	0.984	0.054
GMM_b	−0.5158 (0.3332)	1.0012 (2.0232)	3029	11685.98***	63	0.297	0.048
FE	0.0690 (0.0774)		4377	0.1794			
GMM_a	−0.2241** (0.9841)		3029	11526.73***	54	0.985	0.056
GMM_b	−0.3577 (0.2322)		3029	11435.49***	58	0.712	0.050
Only establishments located in East Germany (with selection control)							
FE	0.2253 (0.1740)	−1.7132* (0.8856)	4126	0.1277			
GMM_a	0.0311 (0.2138)	−0.7750 (1.0062)	2956	2256.36***	50	0.108	0.728
GMM_b	0.2673 (0.3879)	−2.5998 (1.7106)	2956	2343.57***	58	0.183	0.761
FE	−0.0881 (0.1013)		4126	0.1260			
GMM_a	−0.1044 (0.1131)		2956	2271.95***	49	0.104	0.727
GMM_b	−0.2598 (0.2334)		2956	2312.60***	53	0.123	0.731

Notes: Robust standard errors in parentheses
* $p<0.1$; ** $p<0.05$; *** $p<0.01$
GMM_a: System GMM exogenous; GMM_b: System GMM predetermined

Two further robustness checks are carried out by running separate regression models for West and East Germany. For this robustness check, all establishments located in Berlin are excluded because it is not possible to assign them to either West or East Germany. For each subsample, one fixed effects specification and two system GMM models are estimated with and without *Share2*. All models for both subsamples include the inverse Mills ration to control for selection into the use of fixed-term employment. The results for the West German subsample are reported in the second part of Table 5.8. In the models with both share variables, only the coefficient for the squared term of share in the first system GMM model is significant at the 5 % level. The respective sign is negative. Excluding *Share2* results in insignificant coefficients for the *Share* variable in all models except the system GMM model treating the share variable as exogenous. In the third part of Table 5.8 the results for the East German subsample are provided. Again no evidence for the expected inverse U-shaped relationship or for a negative relationship is found. Including both share variables, all coefficients have the expected sign, but only one coefficient of *Share2* is significant. Excluding *Share2* leads to insignificant coefficients in all models for the East German subsample. So in general the robustness checks confirm our findings that there is no evidence for an inverse U-shaped relationship between the intensity fixed-term contracts are used and labor productivity. Evidence for a negative relationship is also not found.

It follows, that our hypothesis of an inverse U-shaped relationship between the share of employees with a fixed-term contract on total work force of an establishment and labor productivity has no support. This result is robust, regardless the estimation method applied or the subsample examined. Moreover, our results also suggest that there is not even a significant relationship between the use of fixed-term employment and labor productivity. However, the analysis has also shown that the selection effect plays a role and ignoring this can potentially lead to false conclusions.

5.5 Conclusion

The importance of fixed-term contracts in filling vacancies, but also in terms of their share on total workforce, is increasing. The aim of this study is to analyze whether, and if so, to what extent, this development improves the productivity of companies. Put differently, is it in the companies' interest to use this instrument as intensively as possible because it promises to increases productivity?

In order to address this question, we review previous findings of labor market and management research. It shows that temporary employment, in general, is used for two reasons: to screen for productive employees and to handle demand fluctuations. In this respect, using fixed-term contract should positively affect productivity. The literature also suggests the existence of demotivating effects if fixed-term workers are used excessively, as well as decreasing firm-specific human capital with an increasing share of fixed-term workers. Based on the theoretical considerations and empirical findings on these effects, we derive the hypothesis of an inverse U-shaped relationship between the share of fixed-term workers on total workforce and productivity.

To test this hypothesis, we use a large dataset containing German establishments and apply several panel data models. The inherent selection problem is taken into account via the inverse Mills ratio and the inverse U-shape is modeled by two variables, the share of fixed-term workers and its square. Yet, the empirical analysis provides no support for the hypothesis. Rather, we find mostly negative coefficients for both variables modeling the share of fixed-term workers on total workforce, with the squared variable being weakly significant in a few estimations. It is then tested whether the relationship is not inverse U-shaped but negative. Again, no significant relationship is found, although the coefficients are still negative. Hence, our study reveals that there is no significant relationship between the use of fixed-term employment and labor productivity in the German case. This is in line with the findings of Kleinknecht et al. (2006) for Dutch firms. Since we see mostly negative coefficients, although not significant, it also partly confirms the findings of Cappellari et al. (2012) for Italy, where the relationship is found to be negative.

Yet, the question arises why there is no relationship found when labor- and management literature point to the negative and positive aspects of this instrument. The reason might be that the majority of fixed-term contracts in Germany are longer than 1 year. Hence, the positive effects of adjusting employment without redundancy costs still exists since a firm can lay off some of the fixed-term works every month (if hired a year before), but it would still have to pay some redundancy costs if it tries to terminate all of them in the event of demand slump. In this respect fixed-term employment is not as flexible as temporary agency work and, thus, the positive effects of increased flexibility are limited. But also the negative effect of lower firm specific human capital only partly apply with job tenures of 1 year, since much of this knowledge is transferred in the first few months. Moreover, since 50 % of fixed-term workers in Germany are offered a permanent contract the screening and motivational aspects may also have only little effects. Overall the positive and negative aspects, discussed in the labor- and management literature only partly apply to fixed-term employment in Germany and, thus, the effects might not be as strong.

However, from a policy perspective, this result remains valid. An increasingly flexible labor market in continental European countries, like Germany, is constantly called for. In order to enhance this flexibility, the use of instruments like fixed-term contracts and temporary agency work was simplified by the government. Although this policy was mainly imposed to reduce unemployment and increase the flexibility of the labor market, positive effects for firms were also expected. The findings of this study show, in line with others, that fixed-term contract do not help firms to increase their productivity. From this perspective, therefore, a further expansion of this form of employment seems to be not necessary.

Chapter 6
Summary and Future Research

This chapter summarizes the main results of this dissertation. In the next section the results of both chapters dealing with the relationship between introducing a product innovation are summarized. The second section of this chapter provides a summary of both chapters analyzing the relationship between temporary employment and firm performance. Finally the last section presents some purposes for future research regarding the relationship between firms' short-run responses to capital and labor market frictions and performance.

6.1 Trade Credit and Innovation Performance

It is argued that the introduction of a product innovation is positively related to trade credit. SMEs introducing a product innovation are more likely to face credit constraints compared to non-innovative ones. Furthermore, innovative firms show higher growth rates and therefore need more short-term finance to finance their growth. Hence, innovative SMEs are expected to have a higher probability to demand for trade credit. There are also arguments why suppliers have an incentive to provide trade credit especially to innovative SMEs. Due to the product innovation the customer may have higher growth in the future. This will lead to higher future sales for the supplier. Hence, the supplier has an incentive to help its innovative customer to cope with short-run liquidity constraints to profit from an increase in future demand. Thus, it is expected that the willingness of a supplier to provide trade credit is higher if the customer has introduced a product innovation. Combining demand and supply side arguments innovative SMEs are expected to have a higher probability to use trade credit as as source of short-term finance compared to non-innovative SMEs.

S. Nielen, *Trade Credit and Temporary Employment*, Contributions to Management Science, DOI 10.1007/978-3-319-29850-4_6

Chapter 2 studies the relationship between the use of trade credit and innovation. The relationship between product innovation and trade credit is empirically examined by using a sample of SMEs from 15 European countries. The results of an econometric analysis confirm a positive relationship between innovation and trade credit. In particular, SMEs with product innovations have a higher probability of using trade credit than other SMEs. Moreover, the results suggest that the effect of product innovation is only statistically significant if SMEs report that access to finance or cost of financing are obstacles for the operation and growth of their businesses. Hence, the results point to the relevance of trade credit as a source of short-term external finance for innovative SMEs which are credit constrained.

Chapter 3 goes more into detail and distinguishes between the demand for and provision of trade credit. It is argued that introducing a product innovation is positively linked with trade credit demand as well as the availability of trade credit from business partners. Using a sample covering SMEs from 24 European countries this relationship is tested empirically. Basically the estimation results confirm both hypotheses. First, SMEs introducing a product innovation have a higher probability to demand for trade credit. Second, the availability of trade credit from business partners is also higher compared to non-innovative SMEs. This relationship is found to be stronger for small and young firms. Hence, the results of this chapter points to the role of trade credit as a source of short-term finance for small and young innovative firms.

6.2 Temporary Employment and Firm Performance

There are three main channels how the use of temporary employment could influence firm performance. The first one is increased labor flexibility. Temporary employment is used to adjust the labor force on fluctuations in product demand. According to this channel the use of temporary employment should be positively related to firm performance. Another possible channel is called screening and motivation. The performance effects of using temporary employment due to screening and motivation depend on the intensity temporary employment is used. A moderate use of temporary employment to screen potential new employees should increase firm performance. If the share of temporary employees is relative high going in line with the substitution of permanent workers with temporary ones both types of workers are less motivated. This should affect firm performance negatively. The last channel is about human capital of temporary employees. Combining the three different channels how the use of temporary employment affect firm performance an inverse u-shaped relationship is expected. A moderate use should increase firm performance due to a higher flexibility and the possibility to screen potential new employees.

Chapter 4 of this dissertation addresses the relationship between the utilization of temporary agency workers by firms and their competitiveness measured by unit labor costs, using a rich, newly built, data set of German manufacturing enterprises.

The analysis is conducted by applying different panel data models while taking the inherent selection problem into account. Making use of dynamic panel data models allows to control for firm specific fixed effects as well as for potential endogeneity of explanatory variables. The results indicate an inverse U-shaped relationship between the extent that temporary agency workers are used and the competitiveness of firms. Estimating separate models for industry groups provide mixed results. The expected inverse U-shaped relationships between the use of temporary agency work and competitiveness is only found for some industry groups.

Chapter 5 empirically analyzes whether the usage of fixed-term employment actually improves firm productivity. To this end, a large data set of German manufacturing firms and various panel data models are used in order to reveal the expected non-linear effect. Thereby the analysis also takes into account distortions that may result from selection into the use of fixed-term employment. The results of the investigation show that there is no significant effect of fixed-term employment on labor productivity when taking into account potential selection effects.

6.3 Purposes for Future Research

The results of this dissertation provide a lot of issues and directions for future research on the relationship between the use of short-term adjustment strategies and performance. The results regarding the relationship between product innovations and trade credit in this dissertation are based on cross sectional data. Future research may make use of panel data if possible to investigate whether the results still hold when taking into account unobserved heterogeneity. Furthermore, more research on the role of trade credit for young firms and start-ups is needed. Young firms and start-ups are often faced with problems to receive finance. Hence, trade credit could play an important role to finance start-ups and help them to survive the early years of their business.

The chapters analyzing the relationship between the use of temporary employment and firm performance focus only on manufacturing firms. In the last years the importance of service industries has increased. Hence, it would be worthwhile to analyze the effects of temporary employment on firm performance for service industries. By doing so, one should distinguish between service sectors like hotels or restaurants and knowledge intensive-business services, because the use of temporary employment should be different in both groups.

Finally, further relationships between trade credit, temporary employment, innovation performance, and firm performance are interesting points for future research. A very interesting research question is how the increasing utilization of temporary employment affects innovation activities of firms. Since the studies of Arvanitis (2005), Giannetti and Madia (2013) and Zhou et al. (2011) provide mixed results regarding the relationship between temporary employment and innovation performance more research on that topic is needed.

References

Addison, J. T., & Surfield, C. J. (2009). Atypical work and employment continuity. *Industrial Relations, 48*(4), 655–683.

Aghion, P., Fally, T., & Scarpetta, S. (2007). Credit constraints as a barrier to the entry and post-entry growth of firms. *Economic Policy, 22*, 731–779.

Albert, C., Carcía-Serrano, C., & Hernanz, V. (2005). Firm-provided training and temporary contracts. *Spanish Economic Review, 7*, 67–88.

Alesina, A., & Perotti, R. (1997). The welfare state and competitiveness. *American Economic Review, 87*(5), 921–939.

Almus, M., & Nerlinger, E. A. (1999). Growth of new technology-based firms: Which factors matter? *Small Business Economics, 13*, 141–154.

Amuedo-Dorantes, C. (2000). Work transitions into and out of involuntary temporary employment in a segmented market: Evidence from Spain. *Industrial and Labor Relations Review, 53*(2), 309–325.

Antoni, M., & Jahn, E. J. (2009). Do changes in regulation affect employment duration in temporary help agencies? *Industrial and Labor Relations Review, 62*(2), 226–251.

Arellano, M., & Bond, S. (1991). Some tests of specification for panel data: Monte Carlo evidence and an application to employment equations. *Review of Economic Studies, 58*, 277–297.

Arellano, M., & Bover, O. (1995). Another look at the instrumental variable estimation of error-components models. *Journal of Econometrics, 68*, 29–51.

Arulampalam, W., Booth, A. L., & Bryan, M. L. (2004). Training in Europe. *Journal of the European Economic Association, 2*(2–3), 346–360.

Arvanitis, S. (2005). Modes of labor flexibility at firm level: Are there any implications for performance and innovation? Evidence for the Swiss economy. *Industrial and Corporate Change, 14*(6), 993–1016.

Atanasova, C. V., & Wilson, N. (2003). Bank borrowing constraints and the demand for trade credit: Evidence from panel data. *Managerial and Decision Economics, 24*, 503–514.

Auer, P., Berg, J., & Coulibaly, I. (2005). Is a stable workforce good for productivity? *International Labour Review, 114*(3), 319–343.

Autor, D. H. (2003). Outsourcing at will: The contribution of unjust dismissal doctrine to the growth of employment outsourcing. *Journal of Labor Economics, 21*(1), 1–42.

Bassanini, A., Nunziata, L., & Venn, D. (2009). Job protection legislation and productivity growth in OECD countries. *Economic Policy, 24*(58), 349–402.

Bastos, R., & Pindado, J. (2007). An agency model to explain trade credit policy and empirical evidence. *Applied Economics, 39*, 2631–2642.

S. Nielen, *Trade Credit and Temporary Employment*, Contributions to Management Science, DOI 10.1007/978-3-319-29850-4

Beck, T., Demirgüc-Kunt, A., & Maksimovic, V. (2005). Financial and legal constraints to growth: Does firm size matter? *Journal of Finance, 60*, 137–177.

Becker, G. S. (1964). *Human capital: A theoretical and empirical analysis, with special reference to education*. New York: National Bureau of Economic Research.

Beckmann, M., & Kuhn, D. (2009). *Temporary agency work and firm performance: Evidence from German establishment-level panel data* (WWZ Discussion Paper 01/09).

Beckmann, M., & Kuhn, D. (2012). *Flexibility vs. screening: The performance effects of temporary agency work strategies* (WWZ Discussion Paper 2012/03).

Bellmann, L., Kohaut, S., & Lahner, M. (2002). *Das IAB-Betriebspanel - Ansatz und Analysepotenziale* (Vol. 250; G. Kleinhenz, Ed.). IAB.

Bentolila, S., & Saint-Paul, G. (1992). The macroeconomic impact of flexible labor contracts, with an application to Spain. *European Economic Review, 36*, 1013–1053.

Bergmann, A., & Mertens, A. (2011). Job stability trends, lay-offs, and transitions to unemployment in West Germany. *Labour, 25*(4), 421–446.

Biais, B., & Gollier, C. (1997). Trade credit and credit rationing. *Review of Financial Studies, 10*, 905–937.

Blundell, R., & Bond, S. (1998). Initial conditions and moments restrictions in dynamic panel data models. *Journal of Econometrics, 87*, 115–143.

Bogetoft, P., & Hougaard, J. L. (2003). Rational inefficiencies. *Journal of Productivty Analysis, 20*(3), 243–271.

Bönte, W., & Nielen, S. (2011). Product innovation, credit constraints, and trade credit: Evidence from a cross-country study. *Managerial and Decision Economics, 32*, 413–424.

Boockmann, B., & Hagen, T. (2008). Fixed-term contracts as a sorting mechanisms: Evidence from job durations in West Germany. *Labour Economics, 15*(5), 984–1005.

Booth, A. L., Dolado, J. J., & Frank, J. (2002a). Symposium on temporary work: Introduction. *The Economic Journal, 112*(480), F181–F188.

Booth, A. L., Francesconi, M., & Frank, J. (2002b). Temporary jobs: Stepping stones or dead ends? *The Economic Journal, 112*(480), F189–F213.

Briggs, D. C. (2004). Causal inference and the Heckman model. *Journal of Educational and Behavioral Statistics, 29*(4), 397–420.

Brouwer, E., Kleinknecht, A., & Reijen, J. O. N. (1993). Employment growth and innovation at the firm level. *Journal of Evolutionary Economics, 3*, 153–159.

Brown, S., & Sessions, J. G. (2005). Employee attitudes, earnings and fixed-term contracts: International evidence. *Review of World Economics, 141*(2), 296–317.

Bryson, A. (2007). *Temporary agency workers and workplace performance in the private sector* (Discussion Paper No. 3, Manpower Human Resources Lab).

Bryson, A. (2013). Do temporary agency workers affect workplace performance? *Journal of Productivty Analysis, 39*, 131–138.

Buddelmeyer, H., & Wooden, M. (2011). Transitions out of casual employment: The Australian experience. *Industrial Relations, 50*(1), 109–130.

Burgess, J., & Connell, J. (2005). Temporary agency work: Conceptual, measurement and regulatory issues. *International Journal of Employment Studies, 13*(2), 19–41.

Caggese, A., & Cunat, V. (2008). Financing constraints and fixed-term employment contracts. *The Economic Journal, 118*, 2013–2046.

Cappellari, L., Aringa, C. D., & Leonardi, M. (2012). Temporary employment, job flows and productivity: A tale of two reforms. *The Economic Journal, 122*, F188–F215.

Carcia-Teruel, P. J., & Martinez-Solano, P. (2007). Short-term debt in Spanish SMEs. *International Small Business Journal, 25*(6), 579–602.

Carcia-Teruel, P. J., & Martinez-Solano, P. (2010). Determinants of trade credit: A comparative study of European SMEs. *International Small Business Journal, 28*(3), 215–233.

Cheng, N. S., & Pike, R. (2003). The trade credit decision: Evidence of UK firms. *Managerial and Decision Economics, 24*, 419–438.

Coad, A., & Rao, R. (2008). Innovation and firm growth in high-tech sectors: A quantile regression approach. *Research Policy, 37*, 633–648.

Cunat, V. (2007). Trade credit: Suppliers as debt collectors and insurance providers. *Review of Financial Studies, 20(2)*, 491–527.
Damiani, M., & Pompei, F. (2010). Labour protection and productivity in EU economies: 1995–2005. *The European Journal of Comparative Economics, 7*(2), 373–411.
Danielson, M. G., & Scott, J. A. (2004). Bank loan availability and trade credit deemand. *The Financial Review, 39*, 579–600.
DeCuyper, N., de Jong, J., Witte, H. D., Isakasson, K., Rigotti, T., & Schalk, R. (2008). Literatur rewiev of theory and research on the psychological impact of temporary employment: Towards a conceptual model. *International Journal of Management Reviews, 10*(1), 25–51.
Dolado, J. J., & Stucchi, R. (2008, November). *Do temporary contracts affect TFP? Evidence from Spanish manufacturing firms* (Discussion Paper No. 3832).
Eichhorst, W., Marx, P., & Thode, E. (2010). *Atypische Beschäftigung und Niedriglohnarbeit - Benchmarking Deutschland: Befristete und geringfügige Tätigkeiten, Zeitarbeit und Niedriglohnbeschäftigung* (I Z A Research Report No. 25).
Emery, G. W. (1984). A pure financial explanation for trade credit. *Journal of Financial and Quantitative Analysis, 19*, 271–285.
Engellandt, A., & Riphahn, R. T. (2005). Temporary contracts and employee effort. *Labour Economics, 12*(3), 281–299.
Felipe, J. (2007). A cautionary note on the interpretation of unit labor costs as an indicator of competitivenes, with reference to the Philippines. *Philippine Journal of Developmen, 34*(2), 2–23.
Fischer, G., Janik, F., Müller, D., & Schmucker, A. (2009). The IAB establishment panel – things users should know. *Schmollers Jahrbuch, 129*(1), 133–148.
Fisman, R., & Love, I. (2003). Trade credit, financial intermediary development, and industry growth. *Journal of Finance, 58*(1), 353–374.
Forde, C., Slater, G., & Green, F. (2008). *Agency working in the UK: What do we know?* (Policy Report no. 2, Centre for Employment Relations Innovation & Change).
Fritsch, M., Goerzig, B., Hennchen, O., & Stephan, A. (2004). Cost structure surveys for Germany. *Schmollers Jahrbuch/Journal of Applied Social Sience Studies, 124*, 557–566.
Gash, V. (2008). Bridge or trap? Temporary workers transitions to unemployment and to the standard employment contract. *European Sociological Review, 24*(5), 651–668.
George, E. (2003). External solutions and internal problems: The effects of employment externalisation on internal workers' attitudes. *Organisational Sience, 14*(4), 386–402.
Gerfin, M., Lechner, M., & Steiger, H. (2005). Do subsidised temporary employment get the unemployed back to work? An economic analysis ot two different schemes. *Labour Economics, 12*(6), 807–835.
Giannetti, C., & Madia, M. (2013). Work arrangements and firm innovation: Is there any relationship. *Cambridge Journal of Economics, 37*, 273–297.
Guiso, L. (1998). High-tech firms and credit rationing. *Journal of Economic Behavior & Organization, 35*, 39–59.
Gundert, S., & Hohendanner, C. (2011). Soziale Teilhabe ist eine Frage von stabilen Jobs. *IAB Kurzbericht, 4*, 1–8.
Hagen, T. (2003). Does fixed-term contract employment raise firms' adjustment speed? Evidence form an establishment panel for West Germany. *Jahrbücher für Nationalökonomie und Statistik, 223*(4), 403–421.
Hall, B. H. (2002, Spring). The financing of research and development. *Oxford Review of Economic Policy, 18*(1), 35–51.
Heckman, J. (1979). Sample selection bias as a specification error. *Econometrica, 47*(1), 153–161.
Heywood, J. S., Siebert, W. S., & Wei, X. (2011). Estimating the use of agency workers: Can family-friendly practices reduce their use? *Industrial Relations, 50*(3), 535–564.
Himmelberg, C. P., & Petersen, B. C. (1994, February). R&D and internal finance: A panel study of small firms in high-tech industries. *The Review of Economics and Statistics, 76*(1), 38–51.
Hirsch, B., & Mueller, S. (2012). The productivity effect of temporary agency work: Evidence from German panel data. *The Economic Journal, 122*, F216–F235.

Houseman, S. N. (2001). Why employers use flexible staffing arrangements: Evidence from an establishment survey. *Industrial and Labor Relations Review, 55*(1), 149–170.

Howorth, C., & Reber, B. (2003). Habitual late payment of trade credit: An empirical examination of UK small firms. *Managerial and Decision Economics, 24*, 471–482.

Huyghebaert, N. (2006). On the determinants and dynamics of trade credit use: Empirical evidence from business start-ups. *Journal of Business Finance and Accounting, 33*(1) & (2), 305–328.

Huyghebaert, N., de Gucht, L. V., & Hulle, C. V. (2007). The choice between bank debt and trade credit in business start-ups. *Small Business Economics, 29*, 435–452.

Hyytinen, A., & Toivanen, O. (2005). Do financial constraints hold back innovation and growth?: Evidence on the role of public policy. *Research Policy, 34*, 1385–1403.

IAB. (2011). IAB-Aktuell 18.02.2011. http://doku.iab.de/aktuell/2011/befristete_beschaeftigung_uebernahme.pdf

Ichino, A., & Riphahn, R. T. (2005). The effect of employment protection on worker effort: Absenteeism during and after probation. *Journal of the European Economic Association, 3*(1), 120–143.

Jahn, E. J. (2010). Reassessing the pay gap for temps in Germany. *Jahrbücher für Nationalökonomie und Statistik, 230*(2), 208–233.

Jain, N. (2001). Monitoring costs and trade credit. *The Quarterly Review of Economics and Finance, 41*, 89–110.

Jaramillo, F., Schiantarelli, F., & Weiss, A. (1996). Capital market imperfections before and after financial liberalization: An Euler equation approach to panel data for Ecuadorian firms. *Journal of Development Economics, 51*, 367–386.

Jones, M. K., Jones, R. J., Latreille, P. L., & Sloane, P. J. (2009). Training, job satisfaction, and workplace performance in Britain: Evidence from WERS 2004. *Labour, 23*(s1), 139–175.

King, G., & Zeng, L. (2001). Logistic regression in rare events data. *Political Analysis, 9*(2), 137–163.

Kleinknecht, A., Oostendorp, R. M., Pradhan, M. P., & Naastepad, C. (2006). Flexible labour, firm performance and the Dutch job creation miracle. *International Review of Applied Economics, 20*(2), 171–187.

Kvasnicka, M. (2003). *Inside the black box of temporary help agencies*. (Discussion papers of interdisciplinary research project 373, No. 2003, 43).

Lagos, R. (2006). A model of TFP. *The Review of Economic Studies, 79*(4), 983–1007.

Lööf, H., & Heshmati, A. (2002). Knowledge capital and performance heterogeneity: A firm-level innovation study. *International Journal of Production Economics, 76*, 61–85.

Mateut, S. (2005). Trade credit and monetary policy transmission. *Journal of Economic Surveys, 19(4)*, 655–670.

McGinnity, F., Mertens, A., & Gundert, S. (2005). A bad start? Fixed-term contracts and the transition form education to work in West Germany. *European Sociological Review, 21*(4), 359–374.

Mertens, A., & McGinnity, F. (2004). Wages and wage growth of fixed-term workers in East and West Germany. *Applied Economics Quarterly, 50*(2), 139–163.

Mertens, A., Gash, V., & McGinnity, F. (2007). The cost of flexibility at the margin. Comparing the wage penalty for fixed-term contracts in Germany and Spain using quantile regression. *Labour, 21*(4/5), 637–666.

Mitlacher, L. W. (2008). Job quality and temporary agency work: Challenges for human resource management in triangular employment relations in Germany. *The International Journal of Human Resource Management, 19*(3), 446–460.

Miwa, Y., & Ramseyer, J. M. (2008). The implications of trade credit for bank monitoring: Suggestive evidence from Japan. *Journal of Economics & Management Strategy, 17*, 317–343.

NG, C. K., Smith, J. K., & Smith, R. L. (1999). Evidence on the determinants of credit terms used in interfirm trade. *Journal of Finance, 54(3)*, 1109–1129.

Nielen, S., & Schiersch, A. (2014). Temporary agency work and firm competitiveness: Evidence from German manufacturing firms. *Industrial Relations, 53*(3), 365–393.

Nilsen, J. H. (2002). Trade credit and the bank lending channel. *Journal of Money, Credit and Banking, 34*(1), 226–253.

Nollen, S. D. (1996). Negative aspects of temporary employment. *Journal of Labor Research, 17*(4), 567–582.

Nunziata, L., & Staffolani, S. (2007). Short-term contracts regulations and dynamic labour demand: Theory and evidence. *Scottish Journal of Political Economy, 54*(1), 72–104.

Ogawa, K., Sterken, E., & Tokutsu, I. (2013). The trade credit channel revisited: Evidence from micro data of Japanese small firms. *Small Business Economics, 40*, 101–118.

Oliveira, B., & Fortunato, A. (2006). Firm growth and liquidity constraints: A dynamic analysis. *Small Business Economics, 27*, 139–156.

Ortega, B., & Marchante, A. J. (2010). Temporary contracts and labour productivity in Spain: A sectoral analysis. *Journal of Productivty Analysis, 34*, 199–212.

Petersen, M. A., & Rajan, R. G. (1994). The benefits of lending relationships: Evidence from small business data. *Journal of Finance, 49*(1), 3–37.

Petersen, M. A., & Rajan, R. G. (1997). Trade credit: Theory and evidence. *Review of Financial Studies, 10*(3), 661–691.

Pfeifer, C. (2005, 01). Beschäftigungsanalysen mit den daten des iab-betriebspanels. tagungsband. beiträge zum workshop des iab und iwh 2005. In I. für Wirtschaftsforschung Halle. Sonderheft (Ed.), (pp. 130–152). L. Bellmann and U. Ludwig.

Picchio, M. (2008). Temporary contracts and transition to stable jobs in Italy. *Labour, 22*(s1), 147–174.

Pike, R., Cheng, N. S., Carvens, K., & Lamminmaki, D. (2005). Trade credit terms: Asymmetric information and price discrimination evidence from three continents. *Journal of Business Finance & Accounting, 32*(5) & (6), 1197–1236.

Puhani, P. A. (2000). The Heckman correction for sample selection and its critique. *Journal of Economic Surveys, 14*(1), 53–68.

Ragnitz, J. (2008, 5). *Leiharbeit in Deutschland: Statistischer Befund und Schlussfolgerungen für die empirische Wirtschaftsforschung* (IFO Dresden bericht).

Rodriguez-Rodriguez, O. M. (2006). Trade credit in small and median size firms: An application of the system estimator with panel data. *Small Business Economics, 27*, 103–126.

Roodman, D. (2009a). How to do xtabond2: An introduction to difference and system GMM in Stata. *The Stata Journal, 9*(1), 86–136.

Roodman, D. (2009b). Practitioner's corner a note on the theme of too many instruments. *Oxford Bulletin of Economics and Statistics, 71*(1), 135–158.

Roper, S. (1997). Product innovation and small business growth: A comparison of the strategies of German, UK and Irish companies. *Small Business Economics, 9*, 523–537.

Rudolph, E. J. J. (2002). *Zeitarbeit teil ii: Voellig frei bis streng geregelt. variantenvielfalt in europa* (IAB Kurzbericht Nr. 21).

Schiersch, A. (2013). Firm size and efficiency in the German mechanical engineering industry. *Small Business Economics, 40*(2), 335–350.

Schmidt, K., & Wuellerich, J. (2011). Der arbeitsmarkt in deutschland, arbeitsmarktberichterstattung – januar 2011: Zeitarbeit in deutschland – aktuelle entwicklungen. (Nuernberg: Bundesagentur fuer Arbeit).

Schumpeter, J. A. (1942). *Capitalism, socialism and democracy*. New York/London: Harper & Row.

Schwartz, R. A. (1974). An economic model of trade credit. *Journal of Financial and Quantitative Analysis 9*(4), 643–657.

Shire, K. A., Mottweiler, H., Schönauer, A., & Valverde, M. (2009). Temporary contracts in coordinated market economies: Evidence form front-line service workplaces. *Industrial and Labor Relations Review, 62*(4), 602–617.

Städele, D., & Müller, D. (2006). *"Codebuch zum IAB-Betriebspanel." FDZ Datenreport.*

Stiglitz, J. E., & Weiss, A. (1981). Credit rationing in markets with imperfect information. *American Economic Review, 71*, 393–410.

Summers, B., & Wilson, N. (2003). Trade credit and customer relationships. *Managerial and Decision Economics, 24*(6) & (7), 439–455.

Tsuruta, D. (2008). Bank information monopoly and trade credit: Do only banks have information about small businesses? *Applied Economics, 40*, 981–996.

Tsuruta, D. (2012). How do small business finance their growth opportunities? The case of recovery from the lost decade in Japan. *Managerial and Decision Economics, 33*, 189–210.

Ughetto, E. (2009). Industrial districts and financial constraints to innovation. *International Review of Applied Economics, 23*, 597–624.

van Ark, B., Stuivenwold, E., & Ypma, G. (2005). Unit labour costs, productivity and international competitiveness. Research Memorandum GD-80, Groningen Growth and Development Centre.

Vidal, M., & Tigges, L. M. (2009). Temporary employment and strategic staffing in the manufacturing sector. *Industrial Relations, 48*(1), 55–72.

Wagner, J. (2000). Firm panel data from German official statistics. *Schmollers Jahrbuch/Journal of Applied Social Sience Studies, 120*(1), 143–150.

Wagner, J. (2010a). Estimated capital stock values for German manufacturing enterprises covered by the cost structure surveys. *Schmollers Jahrbuch/Journal of Applied Social Sience Studies, 130*(3), 403–408.

Wagner, J. (2010b). The research potential of new types of enterprise data based on surveys from official statistics in Germany. *Schmollers Jahrbuch/Journal of Applied Social Sience Studies, 130*(1), 133–142.

Wang, R., & Weiss, A. (1998). Probation, layoffs, and wage-tenure profiles: A sorting explanation. *Labour Economics, 5*(3), 359–383.

Wasmer, E. (2006). General versus specific skills in labor markets with search frictions and firing costs. *The American Economic Review, 96*(3), 811–831.

Zhou, H., Dekker, R., & Kleinknecht, A. (2011). Flexible labor and innovation performance: Evidence from longitudinal firm-level data. *Industrial and Corporate Change, 20*(3), 941–968.

Zuehlke, S., Zwick, M., Scharnhorst, S., & Wende, T. (2004). The research data centres of the federal statistical office and the statistical offices of the laender. *SchmollersSchmollers/Journal of Applied Social Sience Studies, 124*, 567–578.

Zwick, T. (2006). The impact of training intensity on establishment productivity. *Industrial Relations, 45*(1), 26–46.

MIX
Papier aus verantwortungsvollen Quellen
Paper from responsible sources
FSC® C105338

If you have any concerns about our products,
you can contact us on
ProductSafety@springernature.com

In case Publisher is established outside the EU,
the EU authorized representative is:
Springer Nature Customer Service Center GmbH
Europaplatz 3, 69115 Heidelberg, Germany

Printed by Libri Plureos GmbH
in Hamburg, Germany